D0204492

# THE REBELLIOUS LIFE
# OF MRS. ROSA PARKS

# THE REBELLIOUS LIFE OF MRS. ROSA PARKS

**YOUNG READERS' EDITION**

ReVisioning History for Young People

## JEANNE THEOHARIS

ADAPTED BY
**BRANDY COLBERT**
AND **JEANNE THEOHARIS**

BEACON PRESS ▪ BOSTON

BEACON PRESS
Boston, Massachusetts
www.beacon.org

Beacon Press books
are published under the auspices of
the Unitarian Universalist Association of Congregations.

24 22 21    8 7 6 5 4 3 2 1

This book is printed on acid-free paper that meets the uncoated paper
ANSI/NISO specifications for permanence as revised in 1992.

Beacon Press's ReVisioning History for Young People series consists
of accessibly written books by notable scholars that reconstruct and
reinterpret U.S. history from diverse perspectives.

Text design and composition by Kim Arney

Excerpts from the poem "Harvest" by Nikki Giovanni
are reprinted here with permission.

*Library of Congress Cataloging-in-Publication Data*

Names: Theoharis, Jeanne, author. | Colbert, Brandy, author.
Title: The rebellious life of Mrs. Rosa Parks / Jeanne Theoharis ; adapted
    by Brandy Colbert.
Description: Young readers' edition. | Boston : Beacon Press, [2020] |
    Includes bibliographical references and index. | Audience: Ages 12+
Identifiers: LCCN 2020011430 (print) | LCCN 2020011431 (ebook) |
    ISBN 9780807067574 (trade paperback) | ISBN 9780807067581 (ebook)
Subjects: LCSH: Parks, Rosa, 1913-2005. | African American women civil
    rights workers—Alabama—Montgomery—Biography—Juvenile literature. |
    Civil rights workers—Alabama—Montgomery—Biography—Juvenile
    literature. | African Americans—Civil rights—Alabama—Montgomery—
    History—20th century—Juvenile literature. | Segregation in
    transportation—Alabama—Montgomery—History—20th century—
    Juvenile literature. | Montgomery (Ala.)—Race relations—Juvenile
    literature. | Montgomery (Ala.)—Biography—Juvenile literature.
Classification: LCC F334.M753 P3883 2020 (print) | LCC F334.M753 (ebook) |
    DDC 323.092 [B]—dc23
LC record available at https://lccn.loc.gov/2020011430
LC ebook record available at https://lccn.loc.gov/2020011431

# CONTENTS

On October 24, 2005, Rosa Parks died in her home in Detroit at the age of ninety-two. Led by Congressman John Conyers, a host of politicians rushed to honor her. She became the first woman, and the first civilian, ever to lie in honor in the US Capitol. President George W. Bush laid a wreath on her coffin. Forty thousand Americans visited the Capitol Rotunda to pay their respects.

Thousands of Americans took off work and school to pay tribute to the civil rights heroine. Parks's body was first flown to Montgomery for a service there, then brought to DC for the honors at the Capitol, and finally returned home to Detroit. Her seven-hour funeral at Greater Grace Temple in Detroit featured speeches by former president Bill Clinton and future president Barack Obama. The streets of Detroit were lined with people who wanted to honor her. About six weeks later, on the fiftieth anniversary of her bus arrest, President Bush signed a bill ordering a statue of Rosa Parks to be installed in the Capitol's National Statuary Hall, the first full-size statue of a Black person ever to be put there.

Yet despite these powerful honors, most of the tributes to her bore only a fuzzy resemblance to who Rosa Parks was and what she believed in. She was referred to incessantly as "quiet" and "not angry"—and her life story was shrunk to one day on the bus.

The *New York Times* referred to her as "the accidental matriarch of the civil rights movement." Bill Frist, the Senate Majority Leader at the time, claimed Parks's refusal to give up her seat on the bus was "not an intentional attempt to change a nation but a singular act aimed at restoring the dignity of the individual." Most placed the events she was involved in firmly in the distant past.

Many politicians wanted to focus on how far the nation had come. Two months before Parks's death, Hurricane Katrina had hit New Orleans. Government inaction and negligence during the storm had left many Black New Orleanians dead, homeless, or stranded. Growing public outrage about the government's response in New Orleans highlighted how deeply racism and economic inequality were embedded in the United States. Many politicians wanted to change the conversation to highlight more positive images of the nation's progress, and a national memorial for Rosa Parks was a good way to do that. Focusing on the inspiring story of a woman denied her seat on the bus now laying in the US Capitol became a way to celebrate Black courage and advancement, papering over the gap between the nation's declaration of liberty and justice for all and the ways it actually treated marginalized communities.

These national honors for Rosa Parks did not do justice to her lifetime of fighting for equality or her beliefs that the United States still had a long way to go. Largely held up as a meek, accidental heroine, she was stripped of her long history of activism, the community of activists she worked with, and her anger at American injustice. In many ways, her larger political beliefs were whitewashed in favor of an endless replay of that photo of her looking out the bus window.

I wrote this book to try to set the record straight—to say that if we're going to honor Rosa Parks, then we have to look at her *whole* life of activism and grapple with who she really was and what her legacy asks of us. Rosa Parks was not a tired lady on the bus who stumbled into history—she was a lifetime freedom fighter. Time and again, she tried to tell people her stand for justice was not a one-day thing and it wasn't just about a bus seat: "Over the years, I have been rebelling against second-class citizenship. It didn't begin when I was arrested." She spent more than half of her life in Detroit, fighting the racism of the North.

And she hated that story about her tired feet: "I didn't tell anyone my feet were hurting. It was just popular . . . because they wanted to give some excuse other than the fact that I didn't want to be pushed around." As she put it, she had a "life history of being rebellious."

When I first began working on this book, people would look at me blankly. *Why did we need another book on Rosa Parks?* Others felt confident we already knew her story, and that the myths about her had been firmly overturned; she wasn't a simple seamstress, they quickly recited, but an NAACP secretary—and besides, she wasn't even the first person arrested for refusing to move. Some even claimed that if Rosa Parks had supported other movements, like Black Power or those fighting against police brutality, "don't you think we would know that already?"

But what I discovered was that even though there were many children's books about her and some of the myths about her had been exposed, no one had written a serious, extensively researched, footnoted book about her. Which meant there was, in fact, so much we didn't know about Rosa Parks—and many myths and omissions had been allowed to stand.

Finding the actual Rosa Parks was not easy. Writing this book (which was first published in 2013 as a detailed biography with nearly 1,500 footnotes and is now adapted here for young adults) required years of research. It meant digging through archives, interviewing dozens of people who knew her, combing through decades of news articles, and reading every interview or letter I could get my hands on. It meant shedding many of the preconceived ideas about the "mother of the civil rights movement."

The idea of the "quiet" Rosa Parks had left people satisfied with a limited sense of her beliefs and contributions. Because Rosa Parks was a woman activist, the narrow way her story was told reflected biased gendered assumptions about what a leader looks like and what issues a person like Rosa Parks would care about. There were assumptions that a person couldn't be shy and believe in Black Power, that the real movement was in the South and not also in the North.

On top of that, Rosa Parks had grown up in a time when talking about her political beliefs could get her killed, and so she learned to be discreet about them. When I started interviewing people who knew her, they told me she never volunteered information; if you didn't ask directly, she would not say. And she was a deeply proud woman who didn't like to talk about herself, so she covered up her own personal pain, particularly the decade of suffering her family endured following her bus stand.

The final difficulty in telling this story was the "master narrative," as longtime civil rights activist Julian Bond calls it, that has grown around the civil rights movement of the 1950s and 1960s. While Rosa Parks and Martin Luther King Jr. are widely embraced today, the story of the movement has been reduced, as Bond puts it, to "Rosa sat down, Martin stood up, then the white folks saw the light and saved the day." Rosa Parks's role is limited to one day when she refused to give up her seat; almost magically a yearlong bus boycott ensued, led by Martin Luther King . . . and the modern civil rights movement was born.

This master narrative has stripped away the power and substance of the civil rights movement—of how much effort it took and how many years people struggled; of how unpopular, imaginative, uncomfortable, and steadfast it was; and of the diverse group of activists who made it possible. This narrative has become a national fable, celebrated in schools and museums, during Black History Month and by national political leaders, but at the same time warping what we know about Parks and the history of the movement.

Telling Rosa Parks's story—because she was active in so many movements across so many decades—thus also provides a broader and more accurate view of the Black freedom struggle across the twentieth century. Her story reveals how a person makes change in a moment and over a lifetime, and what is entailed in the struggle for racial equality—a history with far greater lessons on how we might work for social justice today.

In the years since my original biography of Rosa Parks came out, I have spoken all around the country, invited by high schools and universities, community organizations, teacher trainings, and civil rights groups excited to hear this fuller, more accurate history of Rosa Parks. Over and over, I have heard from students how cheated they feel that they hadn't learned her real story before. Many, many people have asked me to write a book on Parks for younger readers. In the past seven years, I have also discovered more about Rosa Parks, in particular because a huge collection of her papers (letters, personal writings, financial records and photographs), which had been caught up in a dispute over her estate, were finally donated to the Library of Congress.

What I have endeavored to do here is to begin the job of going behind the icon of Rosa Parks to show the scope of her life and political activism in Montgomery and Detroit. This book is different from my original biography—in part because I've learned more about Rosa Parks and also because I've learned much from talking to young people around the country about what resonates in her story. I've realized how much the myths about Parks and the civil rights movement cloud the ways she and the civil rights movement are understood and how important it is to unpack them.

Having started my career more than two decades ago as a high school teacher, I know how much young people crave serious, in-depth African American history (not just posters during Black History Month). Now that I teach African American history and politics in college, most of my students tell me they wished they had learned this material earlier. And having done many workshops with teachers, I've heard how much they desire serious, rigorous books to challenge the problematic narratives and silences found in textbooks. This is my attempt to try to meet that need.

A warning: this book contains stories of brutal violence, including sexual violence. These instances were important to include because one strand of Rosa Parks's lifelong activism was to expose and challenge white brutality against Black people and white men's rape of Black women. Mrs. Parks believed that no matter how small or powerless a person might feel, it was important to call out oppression, and part of what hurt young people were the silences and lack of action by adults.

Her antiviolence work ranged from her own personal experiences challenging sexual aggression to the antirape campaigns she helped build throughout her life seeking justice for women such as Recy Taylor and Joan Little. She fought to challenge the lynching of Emmett Till, the execution of Jeremiah Reeves, and the police killings of three teenagers at the Algiers Motel in Detroit. At the same time, she understood what trauma did to a person—this violence and disregard weighed on one's soul and ability to stay balanced and healthy. Her own beloved, Raymond, had suffered a nervous breakdown during the boycott because he and Rosa had been besieged by death threats and were unable to find work. She compared the trauma of white supremacy to the trauma of war. There was nothing weak or weird to finding it gut-wrenching and hard—and she explicitly refused to normalize the ability to constantly get through oppression.

Also, a word on naming: I refer to Rosa Parks throughout the book as "Rosa," "Parks," and "Mrs. Parks"—and have chosen to use "Mrs. Rosa Parks" in the title. Young adult books typically use the person's first name to be more personal, and scholarly books typically use the last name to be more formal—so I use both here. But I also use "Mrs. Parks" because the title was a form of respect that many white people of the time routinely denied Black women—and thus, it is the way that most people who knew and respected Rosa Parks referred to her. It is what she preferred to be called. Using the "Mrs.," then, does more than mark her marital status. It is meant to add a degree of dignity and formality, to remind us of this history and to refer to her as we might have done if we'd gotten to know her ourselves.

# CHAPTER ONE

# A (SHY) REBEL IS BORN

Rosa Parks's spirit of resistance began early, and it began at home. In fact, she credited her mother and grandfather for her "spirit of freedom," as they made clear that she "should not feel, because of my race or color, inferior to any person."

Rosa Louise McCauley was born on February 4, 1913, in Tuskegee, Alabama. She was named for her grandmothers on both sides, Rose and Louisa. Rosa's parents had both been raised in Alabama; her mother, Leona Edwards, was from a small town called Pine Level, and her father, James McCauley, grew up a little over an hour south of there, in Abbeville.

Leona was a schoolteacher, but she stopped teaching when she became pregnant with Rosa. She didn't do much to hide how isolated and lonely she felt as a new mother. Rosa remembered that "she always talked about how unhappy she was."

James continued working as a skilled carpenter and stonemason, which required him to leave home for long stretches of time. Leona wasn't happy about this and urged him to find work at the Tuskegee Institute, a historically Black college and university (HBCU) nearby. James wasn't interested, though, and continued to spend most of his time on the road.

When Rosa was two years old, her little brother, Sylvester, named for their maternal grandfather, was born. Shortly after, James left the family for good. Leona was tired of raising her children alone, so she packed up their belongings and moved them to live with her parents back in Pine Level. So, Rosa grew up without her father, but she was raised in a house full of love, surrounded by three generations: her mother, grandparents, and great-grandfather.

Both of Rosa's grandparents had been enslaved. Her grandfather, who was born to a mother who'd been impregnated by the slave owner's son, had endured a traumatic childhood. Brought up battling violence and near starvation, he had, Rosa said, a "somewhat belligerent attitude toward white people." And because he looked white, he used this privilege to say and do things that would "embarrass and agitate white people."

Leona returned to teaching after James left the family. Schools in Alabama were segregated, as they were across the country, but instead of employing almost all white teachers, Black schools in Alabama frequently hired Black educators. They often weren't treated well, though, and it wasn't easy to get a job as a Black teacher, so for years, Rosa's mother had to work at a school in a town called Spring Hill, two hours away from their home in Pine Level. Leona stayed in Spring Hill during the week, only coming home on weekends. Despite her grandparents' love and care, Rosa had a difficult time with her mother being away so long, one time saying that she and Sylvester didn't have "a mamma or no papa either."

The McCauley-Edwards family had high expectations in their household. Rosa learned the importance of self-respect, which, in her home, meant acting respectable *and* demanding the same respect from others. Rosa's grandfather Sylvester Edwards was proud and politically aware. He supported the Black nationalist leader Marcus Garvey. Born and raised in Jamaica, Garvey founded the Universal Negro Improvement Association before he immigrated to the United States in 1916. Garvey and the organization were focused on Black pride and self-sufficiency, the founding of independent Black businesses, and the idea that Black Americans should return to Africa. Rosa's grandfather admired Garvey's strong message of Black pride and independence.

■ ■ ■

There was an increase of white violence against Black people after World War I. Although Black soldiers had endangered their lives fighting for their country, many white people believed they needed to be "put back in their place" when they returned home from the war. That summer after the war ended became known as Red Summer. Many white people didn't want Black Americans to get ideas about freedom and equality—even though the United States was their home, too, and they'd risked their lives fighting for it.

Violence from the terrorist group the Ku Klux Klan worsened in Pine Level during this time. Rosa's grandfather, who had known the horrors of white violence since

Early Childhood
Incidents and experiences

Deserted by father at 2½ years,
shortly before brother's birth.
Mother was with her semi invalid parents
Greatgrandfather's playing with my
brother and me. He was an ex-slave
of Scotch-Irish descent, African
ancestry either remote or non existant
He died when I was six years old.
Mother taught school in the rural community
where we lived
K K K moved through the country
burning negro Churches, schools, flogging
and killing. Grandfather stayed
up to wait for them to come to
our house. He kept his shot
gun within hand reach
at all times. My aunt, a widow,
and her five small children came
to our house at night. We could
not undress and go to bed at night.
The doors and windows were
boarded and nailed tight from the
inside. I stayed awake many

Rosa Parks's writing on her grandfather protecting
their home from Klan violence

his days as an enslaved child, refused to be intimidated.
Instead of hiding from fear, after nightfall he'd set up shop
on the front porch with a shotgun; the family slept in their
clothes so they could be ready to run in case of attack.
Sometimes six-year-old Rosa would sit vigil with him on
the porch. "I wanted to see him kill a Ku Kluxer," she
said. Her fierce determination started early and at home.

Rosa was a lifelong reader, in part because her mother taught her how to read—along with how to do math—before she was even old enough to attend school. "I don't even remember [a time] when I didn't read," she said. The school for Black children in Pine Level was bare bones, consisting of "a meager one-room, unpainted shack with wooden shutters and no windows." Black children in the South attended school for only six months out of the year since so many worked on farms and in the fields to help provide for their families. White students, however, attended classes for nine months, most unencumbered by the extra work-load their Black peers took on.

Rosa's mother, Leona McCauley

White children, in general, were offered a better education and more convenient circumstances. They had the luxury of a school bus, while Rosa and her friends had to walk to school. When Rosa was very young, the town used money from everyone's taxes to build a nice new school for white children. Black people, however, were on their own—they "had to build and heat their own schools without the help of the town or county or state."

Meanwhile, Rosa's mother was still teaching in Spring Hill and other Black church schools around the state, which often took her away from the family during the week. Teaching could be dangerous work for Black people; the Ku Klux Klan would sometimes travel around the county, attacking and burning down Black schools. When a job at Rosa's school in Pine Level opened up, her mother took the job, finally able to be close to her family Monday through Friday.

As a kid, Rosa was often sick. Medical care was costly, and it took years for her family to save enough money to have her tonsils removed. Since she was home sick a lot, she read a lot. One of the books she read, likely without her family knowing, was called *Is the Negro a Beast?* by William Gallo Schell. In the book, Schell argued against the popular theory that Black people were beasts—and, therefore, fit for slavery—but he still believed Black people were inferior to white people. Rosa was devastated after reading the book, realizing that much of America did not consider Black people to be "complete human beings."

She wanted to prove that Black inferiority was a myth, that Black people were not unintelligent until proven otherwise. But she felt overwhelmed: How would she do this? Discovering Black history in school provided the answer. Rosa said, "I read everything I could, first in school, and then later in magazines." She educated herself on the long history of Black intelligence and innovation, which clearly proved Schell wrong. But Rosa was bothered by how this history was buried; the achievements of Black Americans were not celebrated or even noted in the same way as those of white Americans. She fought the rest of her life to change this.

Rosa found solace in church as a child. Attending services was "one of the events I could look forward to." The Christian faith was proof to Rosa that God supported freedom for all people—and if God believed in equality, shouldn't all of his believers do the same?

Being Black in Alabama in the 1920s meant trying to live a normal life while also knowing danger could be lurking around every corner. It was normal to not only fear but also to *expect* violence from white people on a daily basis. Figuring out how to negotiate this was a constant struggle. Rosa may have been shy, but at key moments she wasn't afraid to stand up for herself: "Maybe the habit of protecting my little brother helped me learn to protect myself." One of her childhood friends pointed out that "nobody ever bossed Rosa around and got away with it."

Once, a young white kid named Franklin was taunting and bothering Rosa and Sylvester. Tired of his bullying, Rosa grabbed a loose brick and "dared him to hit me." Franklin "thought better of the idea and went away." Rosa later recounted the incident to her grandmother. To her surprise, her grandmother got angry at her for being so bold. Scared for her safety, she scolded Rosa, saying she was "too high-strung" and that she shouldn't be talking "biggety to white folks."

Lynching was a serious threat to Black people, and her grandmother warned Rosa that if she continued to stand up for herself, she'd become one of its victims before she was grown. Rosa felt betrayed by her grandmother, and, furious, she argued back, "I would be lynched rather than live to be mistreated [and] not be allowed to say 'I don't like it.'"

Her grandmother was only trying to protect Rosa, to keep her from being targeted and attacked—or even killed. But Rosa didn't like that she was being told to keep quiet and put up with unfair treatment, especially not by someone who understood how dehumanizing it was to be threatened and not defend yourself.

She would struggle with this balance for the rest of her life. "Whites would accuse you of causing trouble when all you were doing was acting like a normal human being

"I would rather be lynched than live to be mistreated and can't say "I don't like it." When I was a very little girl, not more than 10 yrs old, I angrily cried these words to my grandmother in answer to a severe scolding she gave me. I happened to quite casually mention that a white boy had met me in the road some days before and had said he would hit me. He made a threatening gesture with his fist at the same time he spoke. I picked up a small piece of brick and drew back to strike him if he should hit me. I was angry, though he seemed to

Rosa Parks's writing about her grandmother's anger after she stood up to a white bully

instead of cringing." Bold action was a way to get people's attention, and this could lead to change—but it was dangerous and could also lead to violence or death. Still, resistance was a way to fight oppression and assert her self-worth.

Rosa's resistance was just getting started.

# CHAPTER TWO

# FOLLOWING RULES
# AND BREAKING SOME TOO

As Rosa was growing up, Black children in Alabama continued to struggle for the same education as their white counterparts.

If you were Black, public schooling stopped at sixth grade, while white children continued on through middle and high school. Appalled by this discrepancy, Rosa's mother, Leona, sent eleven-year-old Rosa to live with her aunt in Montgomery, Alabama, and enrolled her in Miss White's Montgomery Industrial School. Coming up with the school's tuition wasn't easy for Rosa's mother. Luckily, after her first semester, Rosa received a scholarship in exchange for dusting, sweeping, and cleaning the classrooms.

All of the students at Rosa's school were Black girls, but the teachers were white, and most were not from Montgomery. The school followed the philosophy of industrial education, meaning that Black children should be educated for a job. This meant the girls were educated in a trade focused on the domestic arts, such as cooking, sewing, and caring for

Miss White's School for Girls

sick people—partly because these were generally the only jobs available to Black women at the time. Rosa learned to operate a sewing machine for the first time at school. Though she was proud of her skills, especially since they helped support her throughout her life, she said, "I didn't feel like I wanted to sew for a living."

The head of the school was strict. Miss White had a long list of forbidden items and activities. Her rules included the following:

- No dancing
- No movies
- No makeup
- No jewelry
- No short hair
- No alcohol

Rosa didn't find it hard to follow those rules. In fact, she was teased for being a "goody two-shoes" because she was such a model student. Her classmate Mary Fair Burks said Rosa never went to the boys' side of the school, like some of the other girls. Another student, Johnnie Carr, said that Rosa was one of the few girls who weren't tempted to dance.

Miss White's school was known for instilling a sense of pride and self-respect in its students, which reinforced what Rosa had already learned at home. She had been taught by her family that "I should not set my sights lower than anybody else just because I was Black"—and the school echoed that lesson.

In addition to domestic arts, Rosa and her classmates learned subjects like English, science, and geography, and they were expected to do well. Many of the young women who attended the school, such as Mary Fair Burks and Johnnie Carr, along with Rosa Parks, went on to lead the fight for civil rights in Montgomery in the following decades.

However, though Miss White valued education for Black girls, many of her decisions and ideas were racist. She refused to hire Black teachers, and Rosa later recalled that once, when the discussion turned to slavery, Miss White said that Black people would "probably still be savages climbing trees and eating bananas" if the slave trade had not happened. Rosa kept her mouth shut at the time, but Miss White's comments were upsetting and offensive. They stayed with Rosa for a long while.

Rosa was shy. And she liked to follow the rules. But she still did not put up with being bullied. One day she was walking home to her aunt's house when a white boy on roller skates pushed her off the sidewalk . . .

. . . and Rosa pushed him back.

The boy's mother threatened Rosa, saying she could send her to jail. Rosa knew that a simple accusation from a white person could mean serious trouble for a Black person. But she also knew she'd only been defending herself. So she told the boy's mother, "I didn't want to be pushed."

Once again, Rosa's family was concerned about her bold spirit and worried it would cause problems, so Rosa moved. Again. This time they sent her to live at a nearby cousin's house so she wouldn't have to walk so far to school—and, thus, avoid potential confrontations with combative white kids. However, Rosa was only able to stay at the school through the end of eighth grade; Miss White had to close the school because of treatment by her fellow white townspeople. They didn't appreciate that she was focused on educating Black girls, and they shunned her and the other teachers. Someone had also set a fire to try to damage the school, making it unsafe.

Rosa transferred to Booker T. Washington Junior High. Then she went on to the lab school at Alabama State College—an HBCU in Montgomery; since there was no high school for Black students in the area, the college had opened its own school, in part to train teachers. Leona wanted Rosa to follow in her footsteps and become a teacher, but Rosa felt "the schools were just too segregated and oppressive." Rosa saw how Black teachers were forced to deal with "humiliation and intimidation" at the hands of racist boards of education and officials, and she said, "It just didn't appeal to me." She felt a different calling: to be a nurse or a social worker.

But just as Rosa was making strides in high school, both her grandmother and mother fell ill. Rosa dropped out in the eleventh grade so she could get a job and help

A young Rosa Parks

care for them. This would be a running theme throughout Rosa's life, as she was constantly forced to balance her personal aspirations with caring for her family.

She began doing domestic work—taking care of a white family's home and child. She made only about four dollars for the whole week, even though she worked seven days a week and sometimes nights too.

One evening Rosa was home watching the baby while the family she worked for went out. A white neighbor named Mr. Charlie came over. Another Black employee, a man named Sam, let Mr. Charlie into the house. Mr. Charlie made himself at home, pouring a glass of whiskey, and then approached Rosa, putting his arm around her waist. Disgusted and fearful, Rosa recoiled.

*What could she do?*

She was small, and Mr. Charlie was a big man. Rosa was terrified. But then she remembered one of her favorite Bible verses, Psalm 27:

> *The Lord is my light and my salvation; whom shall I fear?*

She promised herself she'd resist Mr. Charlie's advances.

"I talked and talked of everything I knew about the white man's inhuman treatment of the Negro," Rosa said. She asked Mr. Charlie why white women weren't good enough for him. She said she wasn't willing to be sexually involved with anyone she couldn't marry and reminded him that interracial marriage was illegal in Alabama. Over and over again, she spoke back to him, refusing and resisting him.

Rosa was angered by Mr. Charlie's actions, but she felt especially betrayed by Sam. He was Black, like her, and he had let Mr. Charlie in to see her. Sam had tricked her, and he showed no regard for her safety. She felt "parceled as a commodity from Negro to white man." Mr. Charlie told Rosa that Sam had given his permission for them to be together. She refused. Then Mr. Charlie said she should be with Sam. Rosa refused this, too, saying she "hated" them both.

Rosa had been raised to tell someone what she was willing to do, and that's what she did with Mr. Charlie. She told him explicitly, "If he wanted to kill me and rape a dead body, he was welcome, but he would have to kill me first."

She kept talking and kept refusing. Finally, she picked up a newspaper and started reading, ignoring him, until "at long last, Mr. Charlie got the idea that I meant no, very definitely no."

Rosa Parks didn't speak about this incident during her lifetime. The only record of it is from her personal papers, which were turned over to an auction house after she died and now are housed at the Library of Congress. She appears to have been written this account about twenty-five years after the incident. When this piece of writing first came to light, some people she was close to said they'd never heard about this incident and thought the writing was fiction, not an actual account. However, no other fiction was ever found among Rosa's writing, and the story corresponds to the domestic work she did at that age, along with the mention of her favorite psalm and her lifelong belief in the right to self-defense.

In the account, Rosa called the white neighbor "Mr. Charlie," but this was likely not his name. "Mr. Charlie" was a slang term Black people used at the time to refer to white people and the ways they wielded their power and preferences. So, the fact that she used this term likely meant she was trying to make a bigger point about the nature of oppression Black women faced.

Although there is no proof that the story is fictional, it may have described one incident or a composite of incidents. Maybe it reflected her experience on this particular occasion, or perhaps it was a fusion of her experiences throughout those years, or perhaps it was an embellished version of what she wished had happened, reflecting all she'd wished she'd said to this man that night.

Whatever happened, the account was a clear and early example of Rosa Parks's philosophy of resistance—that each person could resist, no matter how small they were. It also zeroed in on the myriad dangers Black women faced in the workplace and beyond. She would later highlight the hypocrisies of "night time integration and daytime segregation"—that white people wanted their schools, water fountains, elevators, restaurants, and other aspects of public life segregated from Black people at the same time that white men wanted—and often forced—Black women for sex.

This climate took its toll, Rosa explained. "It was not easy to remain rational and normal mentally in such a setting."

# CHAPTER THREE

# INTRODUCING RAYMOND PARKS—"THE FIRST REAL ACTIVIST I EVER MET"

**W**hen she was eighteen, Rosa met someone who showed her a way forward.

A friend introduced her to Raymond Parks. Raymond was instantly intrigued by Rosa. But, at first, Rosa wasn't initially attracted to the twenty-eight-year-old barber. Raymond was so light skinned that he could pass for white, "except he didn't have white people's hair."

Like so many Black people in the South at that time, Raymond had endured a difficult childhood. Born in Wedowee, Alabama, he'd had to forgo formal education because there were so few Black people in his town and the nearest school for Black children was too far away for him to attend. He was also responsible for caring for his sick mother and grandparents, and often "didn't have food, or shoes at the time."

Raymond Parks, 1947

Still, Raymond had learned to read with the help of his mother; once he learned, he loved it. He became an avid reader of Black writers and Black newspapers. He was so knowledgeable about current events and history that most people assumed he was college educated. After his mother died and his caretaking responsibilities subsided, Raymond moved in with a cousin. When he was twenty-one, he finally got the opportunity to attend Tuskegee Institute, where he learned how to be a barber.

After they met, Raymond wanted to see Rosa again and started asking people where she lived. They wouldn't tell him, because they looked at his light skin and assumed he was white, which would mean trouble for Rosa. But he persisted. Driving out by the McCauley residence and seeing her mother, who looked like Rosa, he inquired about where he might find this Rosa McCauley. Leona invited him into their home—but Rosa hid in the bedroom. After he'd been talking to her mother for some time, Rosa broke through her shyness and came out to join the conversation.

This was the first of many visits from Raymond, and he and Rosa began "going on rides to different places and talking about the world." Rosa had never discussed racial issues so honestly with anyone outside of her family, and she was awed by Raymond's bold thinking. Raymond was a man of action and looked for ways he could change the world. She loved how Raymond—or

"Parks," as she called him—stood up for himself and, like her grandfather, wasn't afraid to speak back to white people. He also drove a red Nash with a rumble seat, which was a statement in 1930s Alabama: not only did he have his own car, but he was a Black man who didn't drive for a white person. It was a clear sign that he was "willing to defy the racists." Like many Black people in Alabama, Raymond also owned a gun.

Raymond "refused to be intimidated by white people," Rosa recalled, "unlike many Blacks, who figured they had to stay under 'Mr. Charlie's heel.'" She called him "the first real activist I ever met."

Raymond enjoyed talking about politics, so much so that his chair at the barbershop often was the site of passionate political discussions. Rosa soaked it all in as she and Raymond spent time together, and she began to understand how the country's system of racial injustice could be challenged through collective ways, not just individual acts. Rosa had begun to think there was "no solution for [those of] us who could not easily conform to this oppressive way of life," but in Raymond, she saw there was a possibility to challenge white supremacy through group action.

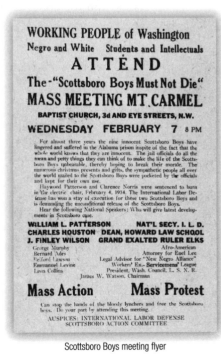

Scottsboro Boys meeting flyer

Raymond had been working to defend a group of nine young Black men when Rosa first met him in 1931. Known as the Scottsboro Boys, they ranged in age from twelve to nineteen, and they'd been "riding the rails," or using the train for free. In the days of the Great Depression, it wasn't unusual for people to hop on a train without paying the fare. The boys got into a fight with a group of white boys who were also riding the rails—and the white boys were forced to leave the train. Furious at being bested by a group of Black boys, the white boys reported them to the police, and they were arrested at the next train stop, in Scottsboro, Alabama. Two young white women were also found to be riding the train for free, and the Black boys were suspected of being up to no good—and the police changed the charge to rape. The court trial was quick, the boys were all found guilty, and every one but the youngest was sentenced to death.

People began working to stop the execution of the Scottsboro Boys and to support them while they were in prison. Raymond was part of that movement, bringing food to the jail for the boys and helping to spread information about meetings to help them. It was difficult to secure legal representation, as most attorneys refused to defend Black people. Even the National Association for the Advancement of Colored People (NAACP), the leading civil rights organization, stayed away from cases like this because they were so controversial and included accusations of sexual misconduct (however false). The International Labor Defense, which was the legal wing of the American Communist Party, agreed to represent the boys.

Being associated with the case was dangerous, so meetings to help the Scottsboro Boys often had to be held in secret. Raymond and his friends would develop signals, such as going to a street corner and tying their shoe a certain way to indicate the date and time for a meeting. They all called each other "Larry" to avoid using their real names.

■ ■ ■

As his relationship with Rosa grew, so did Raymond's love for her determined spirit, as well as her calm and sensible demeanor. He also loved her hair. Though she always wore it up in braids or buns in public, Rosa's hair was long and wavy, and she kept it that way for the rest of her life—even after Raymond died. More than a decade after his death, Rosa took her hair down when she was with the writer Alice Walker, who was "stunned," according to Parks.

"My hair was something my husband dearly, dearly loved about me," Parks told Walker. "I never wear it down in public." Aware of the racial politics of hair, the way she wore her hair reflected the different ways she approached her private and public selves—to Rosa, certain things were only meant for herself and her family.

Rosa soon realized that Raymond was the love of her life, and they married on December 18, 1932, at her mother's house in front of a small group of family and close friends. In her poem "Nikki Rosa," poet Nikki Giovanni wrote "Black love is Black wealth." Rosa agreed. Raymond's support, his caretaking, and his commitment to justice would sustain her throughout their life together.

Raymond encouraged Rosa to return to school, which is what she'd wanted to do ever since she'd been forced to drop out. So, with Raymond's support, Rosa finished high school in 1933, a huge accomplishment at the time. Statistics show that, in 1940, only seven out of every one hundred Black people graduated from high school, so Rosa was very proud of her diploma. She never got to attend college, even though it was one of her "greatest desires."

It was hard, if not impossible, for Black women to get office work in the South, and Rosa had a hard time finding stable employment. She started out as a nurse's assistant at Saint Margaret's Hospital, then moved on to work as a presser at a tailor's shop; during World War II, she worked at Maxwell Air Force Base. Sometimes she had to return to doing domestic work for white families to make money.

Though Rosa was in a loving relationship and armed with a high school diploma, racism loomed large. Schools were deeply segregated and unequal, job discrimination was rampant, and the law did not apply equally to Black and white people. In day-to-day interactions, Black people were still expected to be cheerful and grateful, no matter the job they had to do. And Black men were expected to steer clear of white women in both social and romantic situations.

After they were married, Rosa joined Raymond in working to free the Scottsboro Boys. They often hosted meetings late into the night, the kitchen table "covered with guns" to protect against any threats to their organizing work. In their first years together, Raymond was the more public activist while Rosa remained behind the scenes, often worried for her husband's safety. However, over the years, these roles would change as Rosa became more involved in public activism and Raymond would frequently support *her* behind the scenes.

Once, when Raymond was away on Scottsboro business, Rosa noticed the police drive slowly back and forth in front of their home, over and over. Sitting on the front-porch swing with a friend, she was so frightened by the police stalking her house that her shaking body made the porch swing tremble. Later that evening, Raymond returned home, sneaking in through the back door. Rosa could finally breathe: "At least they didn't get him that time."

Despite constant threats, the work to save the boys continued. Raymond told Rosa he wouldn't sleep "until they were free."

# THE NEWEST MEMBER OF THE NAACP

World War II brought great turmoil to the United States—and the world—in the 1940s. Millions of Americans had joined the fight against the fascism and racism of Germany, Italy, and Japan, known as the Axis Powers—including a million Black servicepeople. President Franklin D. Roosevelt told the country the war was about freedom. But Black people could not ignore the contradiction of helping to preserve freedom abroad while being treated unequally in the United States.

This racism extended to other people of color and ethnicities, as well. President Roosevelt's Executive Order 9066 gave the military the power to remove whomever it considered a threat to the country. The military decreed that nearly 120,000 Japanese Americans living on the West Coast would be put into internment camps—though more than two-thirds of them were US citizens. They were forced to leave their lives behind, including all of their belongings, and sent to live in inhumane makeshift camps. Japanese Americans were imprisoned in these internment camps for years, and, when they were finally allowed to return home, most people were not able to reclaim their property, farms, or fishing boats. Much of their property was taken by their white neighbors or businesses, who viewed Japanese Americans as an economic threat.

Rosa Parks did not like this double standard. Her brother, Sylvester, along with many other Black people as well as many Latinx people and many Japanese Americans, were courageously serving their country during the war overseas. But most Black people weren't able to vote at home. Literacy tests, poll taxes, and a host of other maneuvers kept most Black people, particularly in the South, off the voter registration rolls. A Black newspaper called the *Pittsburgh Courier* organized a campaign for Black people across the nation called the "Double V": victory at home (against discrimination and racial inequality in the United States) and victory abroad (against the fascism of the Axis powers). Some Black people believed in the mission so much that they got tattoos of the Double V.

The US government did not support the "Double V" campaign—especially since it highlighted the country's mistreatment of its own citizens—and called it "un-American." The FBI tried to stop Black newspapers from publishing, taking such measures as rationing their newsprint.

Rosa wanted to become more involved in pushing for change during this tumultuous time. She also wanted to vote. And after she saw a picture in a local Black newspaper of a Montgomery NAACP brance meeting, she was inspired. Pictured there, at the meeting, was Johnnie Carr, one of her classmates from Miss White's school. Rosa hadn't known that women could be part of the local chapter, though she was familiar with the organization.

The NAACP was founded in 1909 to fight for the constitutional rights of Black people, who were subject to growing segregation, an increased number of lynchings, and restricted voting rights. Both Black and white people formed the group, which pursued legal campaigns and political advocacy. The NAACP would become the leading civil rights organization of the twentieth century, with chapters forming around the nation. The Montgomery NAACP was founded in 1918, just after the end of the First World War.

Though Raymond had joined their local branch in the 1930s, he didn't want Rosa to attend the meetings; he said it was too dangerous. But he also had his own problems with the way the Montgomery branch was run. He didn't like the way the middle-class members seemed to look down on a working-class barber like himself, and he felt the organization had grown complacent. They didn't share his commitment to action, so he had stopped going to meetings.

Rosa, however, attended her first NAACP meeting in 1943 and decided to join the branch's efforts. She was one of about a dozen people in attendance—and the only woman—and so the men asked her to take notes. She'd happened to come during a branch election, and because she was "too timid to say no," she was elected secretary on her first day. Many women in Montgomery were dues-paying members of the national NAACP but weren't involved in the local chapter. Rosa set an example by becoming active at the local level, even inspiring her mother to join the Montgomery branch.

Rosa was adamant about registering to vote and made her intentions known. So, a man named E. D. Nixon, who was the local leader of the Brotherhood of Sleeping Car Porters (BSCP) and was leading the local drive for Black voter registration, stopped by her apartment to drop off materials about registering to vote.

Edgar Daniel Nixon, known as E.D., was born on July 12, 1899, and grew up with seven siblings. He went to school for "only about eighteen months of [his] entire life" and worked multiple hard-labor jobs until he was employed as a sleeping car porter.

After the Civil War, the Pullman Company, which built and ran trains, began hiring formerly enslaved Black men as porters because George Pullman, the company's owner, believed they would be the best servants. Porters were responsible for serving white passengers on overnight trains, including making sure they were comfortable, plumping pillows, and taking orders. The white customers often showed little respect, treating the porters as servants and calling them all "George" (referring to the Pullman company's owner). Despite the belittling treatment, the work was steady and the pay was regular, so Black men were eager to find these jobs.

In the 1920s, porters decided they should try to get better wages and more respectful working conditions— which meant they'd need to form a union. The Pullman Company wasn't happy about it. In fact, in 1928, when Nixon's boss learned he'd attended his first union meeting, he threatened to fire him. Nixon had found his first meeting to be "like a light" had turned on. He wasn't about to stop, so he told his boss he'd hired a lawyer and would "drag 'em into court" if he had to. Luckily, Nixon's boss didn't know he was only bluffing and left Nixon alone. Despite their hardships (many porters were fired for their union work), the porters succeeded in creating a union, which was recognized in 1937 after a new law passed that protected Americans trying to form a union. Nixon founded the Montgomery BSCP branch in 1938.

The first meeting of E. D. Nixon and Rosa Parks—a partnership that would change the face of American history—took place in her apartment. Nixon came by to speak to her about registering to vote and, seeing her interest, left a book on the subject for her to read. Meeting Nixon, like meeting Raymond, changed what Rosa saw as possible. She was drawn to Nixon's activism, which expanded her views on liberation and ways to fight racial injustice. In him, she found a comrade who refused to live within the confines of American racism. She felt less alone.

Their first focus was voter registration. Nixon knew there was strength in numbers, and he felt that organizing a group of Black people to vote together would be the best way to tackle the issue of the "hostile" voter registration board, which made voting difficult for Black people. Some ways the board (and voter registration offices across the South) attempted to obstruct voting were these:

- Making people have to take a test when they came in to register and then giving a different test to Black people than was given to white people, with obscure questions about the state constitution or that were completely nonsensical (like "How many bubbles are there in a bar of soap?")

- Opening the registration books only at certain times and telling would-be voters who showed up the rest of the year "If you didn't know when that was, you missed your chance"
- Requiring a letter from a white person to vouch for a Black person who wanted to register to vote
- Running the names of registered voters in the newspaper to incite retaliation against Black potential voters from those who did not believe in equal voting rights
- Making people pay poll taxes starting from the year they were eligible to register to vote

Rosa first tried to register to vote in 1943, though she was unable to go with the group Nixon had organized. She did not pass the test. She tried again the next year and was surprised to see two white women also waiting to register to vote. This was unusual, as officials typically had Black and white people register at different times, which would ensure the Black people didn't see the better treatment given to white people. The registrar motioned to the white women to wait, indicating that she would help them once Rosa left. Once again, Parks did not pass.

In 1945, for the third year in a row, she tried to register to vote. She was tired of getting the run-around for what was her right as an American citizen, and she was considering filing a lawsuit if she again walked away unsuccessful. So, in view of the registrar, Rosa decided to write down all the questions she was given, along with all her answers, to document what happened. A decade before she made her historic stand on the bus, Rosa Parks's fierce determination was clear.

The registrar realized what Rosa was doing and didn't want trouble—and so Rosa received a letter in the mail that confirmed she was now registered to vote.

Even though she'd passed the test, there was another hurdle to cross: the poll tax. Citizens were required to pay poll taxes not just for the year they registered but for all the years dating back to when they were first eligible to vote. Mrs. Parks was thirty-three years old when she was finally able to register, and the voting age was twenty-one at that time. She was forced to pay twelve years of back poll taxes, which totaled $18 (the tax was $1.50 per year), even though she'd wanted to vote all those years and hadn't been able to. This was a huge sum for a working-class family like the Parkses.

Rosa and Raymond scraped together the money to pay the poll tax, and she finally cast her first vote in 1945. She voted for Jim Folsom, who was running for Alabama governor. However, Rosa was one of the few Black people in Montgomery to vote that year. Even her husband, Raymond, had not succeeded in getting registered.

■    ■    ■

Voting rights were a big concern for Black people, but so was the lack of protection against white violence. The police were quick to arrest Black people—or do even worse to them—when they were accused of crimes, but the police and the courts typically ignored it when white people committed crimes against Black people, including assault, rape, or even murder. Black people knew the laws weren't meant to protect them. This was especially clear when it came to the case of a young Black woman named Recy Taylor.

In 1944, twenty-four-year-old Taylor was walking home from a church meeting near Abbeville, Alabama. Six white men pulled up next to her and forced Taylor into their car at gunpoint. After driving her to an isolated area, they raped her—also at gunpoint. Then Taylor was blindfolded, dropped off in the middle of town, and threatened with murder if she told anyone what had happened to her. Taylor refused to be intimidated, though, and reported the crime to the police.

They did nothing.

The Parks family learned about the case from other organizers who'd been fighting for justice in the Scottsboro case, including a white woman named Carolyn Ballin. Ballin had heard about what happened to Recy Taylor and tried to visit her home, but the sheriff had kicked Ballin out of town at gunpoint. Furious about what had happened to Taylor, Rosa and the Montgomery NAACP decided to investigate. Rosa traveled a hundred miles south down to Abbeville, where her father had grown up and where she still had family, to see about the case.

To bring attention to the case, Rosa, Nixon, Johnnie Carr, Rufus Lewis (another NAACP activist who was working on voter registration with Nixon), and other Montgomerians worked with a group called the Committee for Equal Justice for Mrs. Recy Taylor. The goal was to pressure Alabama governor Chauncey Sparks to charge the men who'd violated Taylor. The committee used the same organizational structure and networks built around the Scottsboro case to get in touch with labor unions,

African American groups, and women's organizations and to encourage them to write the governor.

This kind of defense work was dangerous. Even the national NAACP stayed away from these sorts of cases. Though Taylor's supporters agreed that she deserved justice, they didn't all share the same political views. Many of the people who were willing to speak out were left leaning: critical of American capitalism and how it thrived on racism. Some were members of the Communist Party of the United States (CPUSA) and thought that US politics and economic structures needed to be overhauled. Many of these people were viewed as dangerous by the government for their outspoken politics, but they were also the ones courageous enough to speak out on cases like Taylor's. People on the left leading the fight for justice for Taylor included notable Black women tied to the CPUSA, like Esther Cooper and Audley Moore, as well as white Communists like Carolyn Ballin.

Their hard work paid off when the *Pittsburgh Courier* ran a story on Taylor's case that October. Well-known Black writers such as Countee Cullen and Langston Hughes, and political leaders including W. E. B. Du Bois, Mary Church Terrell, and Adam Clayton Powell Jr. joined the Committee for Equal Justice for Mrs. Recy Taylor.

Their efforts resulted in hundreds of letters flooding Governor Sparks's office from across the country. But the governor did nothing, and it soon became clear that the men who'd attacked Taylor would not be charged for their crime. Taylor's supporters feared for her safety in Abbeville, so Nixon and Parks helped the Taylor family move to Montgomery for a while and find work.

## Alabama Committee for Equal Justice
P. O. BOX 1589, BIRMINGHAM, ALABAMA

Hon. Chauncey Sparks,
Governor of Alabama
State Capitol
Montgomery, Alabama
Dear Governor Sparks:

   I wish to commend you for the action you have so far taken on the Recy Taylor case of Abbeville, Alabama. As a citizen of Alabama, I urge you to use your high office to reconvene the Henry County Grand Jury at the earliest possible moment. Alabamians are depending upon you to see that all obstacles, which are preventing justice in this case, be removed. I know that you will not fail to let the people of Alabama know that there is equal justice for all of our citizens.

   Respectfully yours,

   *Rosa L. Parks*
   *22 mill St. montgomery 5 Ala.*

Parks signed a card to Governor Sparks on the Recy Taylor case.

E. D. Nixon's work on the Taylor case, along with his desire to make the Montgomery NAACP chapter more politically active, spurred his decision to run for branch president in 1945. His ideals were supported by a small group of activists including Parks, Carr, and Rufus Lewis, who wanted a chapter more focused on activism. Nixon won, and Mrs. Parks was elected secretary once again. With the new leadership in place, the Montgomery branch joined forces with chapters in Birmingham and Mobile to form a state conference of NAACP branches in 1945; together, they would work to develop solutions and strategies to fight racism across Alabama.

   Rosa's old friend Johnnie Carr was part of these efforts. Two years older than Rosa, Johnnie had been forced to abandon her education when Miss White's school shut down. She'd taken on domestic work, then worked as a nurse, and then moved up to a job with the Atlanta Life Insurance Company. Her civil rights work

Johnnie Carr, Rosa Parks, and E. D. Nixon at an NAACP meeting, 1949

was just getting started, and as it would for Rosa, it
would last a lifetime. Together, they spent years building
the NAACP chapter, laying the ground for a movement to
flower in Montgomery.

Nixon, Parks, Carr, and a small number of other
Montgomery NAACP members strived to transform their
chapter into one that challenged the various forms of injustice in the city, including inequities in voter registration
and the criminal justice system, and the segregation of
city life, from schools to buses to libraries. Her NAACP
colleagues were crucial to Rosa maintaining her per-
sistence during these years. She was often overwhelmed
by the ways that she "could not easily conform to this
oppressive way of life." Working with a group of people
who refused to give in to racial injustice lessened some of
that frustration and made her feel less alone.

Nixon saw Parks as an invaluable grassroots organizer and office manager. She was a voracious reader and kept up with various Black newspapers, which helped the branch stay aware of broader issues. But Nixon held sexist ideas about gender roles. He'd sometimes say, "Women don't need to be nowhere but in the kitchen." Rosa challenged him, asking, "Well, what about me?" And E.D. replied, "I need a secretary and you are a good one."

Rosa was able to push past these comments to help achieve the group's goals of inciting change, sometimes laughing at E.D. when he made such sexist remarks. And though he held some troubling ideas about women's roles, he was also one of her greatest supporters over the next few decades. Still, Parks was aware that Nixon never fully acknowledged her intellectual talents or organizing skills. And this would shape the roles he thought she could play in the future.

# CHAPTER FIVE

# ORGANIZING IN THE FACE OF OPPOSITION

The Montgomery chapter of the NAACP was divided.

The middle-class members didn't like the more political direction Rosa Parks and E. D. Nixon were headed with the branch—so they took action. They wrote to the national NAACP office to have Nixon removed as president, calling him a "dictator" whose "politicking" they didn't like.

This tension wasn't unusual, as many Black Montgomerians didn't share the same vision for the organization and for direct challenge, seeing it as dangerous and foolhardy. Some members wanted the NAACP chapter to be more of a social club and saw themselves as better qualified to be leaders than working-class members like Nixon, who had little education. They worried about retaliation for the politicking, especially as some had more money than others and worried about losing the jobs they'd

Rosa and Raymond Parks, left side, third and fouth chair,
likely at a Montgomery NAACP branch meeting

worked hard to obtain. Others wanted the chapter's
political advocacy to have more of a national focus and
keep it away from local issues (and thus potential local
retaliation).

Nixon was disturbed by this pressure to pull away
from politics. So he pushed harder, trying at one point
to restrict local branch elections only to people who'd
registered to vote. He wanted the chapter to be shaped by
people who'd shown courage and political commitment.
This did not go over well with the members, who persuaded the national office to reject the suggestion.

The middle-class members of the Montgomery branch
actively resisted Nixon's leadership, explicitly campaign-
ing against him. They also decided to run a candidate

against Parks because they now wanted a "male secretary with a firm hand."

Nonetheless, Nixon and Parks were both reelected to their posts in the 1946 branch election. And under Nixon's leadership, membership in the Montgomery NAACP increased from 861 people to 1,600. Still, most Black people in Montgomery saw the local chapter as too dangerous. Even Rosa's mother worried. According to Nixon, "Her mother said the white folks was going to lynch us, her and me both. Mrs. Parks and I were in the NAACP when other Negroes were afraid to be seen with us."

However, Nixon and Parks found encouragement when they traveled to an NAACP workshop in Atlanta, led by Ella Baker. Serving as the NAACP's director of branches, Baker traveled the country, working to cultivate local leadership in NAACP chapters. Parks was inspired by the possibilities Baker outlined and by her philosophy that many people could be leaders and organizers for change. She noticed the director's "funny and smart and strong" qualities.

Ella Baker was born in 1903 in Norfolk, Virginia, and raised in a family that encouraged her political spirit. After an education at Shaw University, a historically Black college in Raleigh, North Carolina, she moved to Harlem and began working for the NAACP in New York City. Baker was promoted to director of branches in 1943 with the intention of equipping Black people with the tools they needed to take on the local problems affecting their communities. Baker believed that "strong people don't need strong leaders," meaning that people could be their own leaders, though most weren't *encouraged* to do so. To be able to challenge the issues affecting the Black community, a wide variety of people had to work together through grassroots organizing.

Parks was greatly inspired by Baker's workshops. Both women placed tremendous emphasis on the importance of local leadership and believed in training young people, who would be the ones to continue fighting the injustice that plagued their community. This belief would inform the work Parks and Johnnie Carr did with the local chapter's young members.

Meeting Ella Baker helped develop Parks's growing sense of her own possibility. Baker became a role model, as Rosa learned how to be a lifelong activist and freedom fighter. Though Baker resigned her position due to the NAACP's refusal to let local branches set the course of the organization, she and Rosa remained friends. Baker would go on to head the Harlem NAACP in the 1950s and help lead the fight against school segregation in New York City. She would often stay at the Parkses' apartment in the Cleveland Court Projects when she visited Montgomery.

■  ■  ■

Cleveland Court was built as a completely segregated housing project for Black families, while the Jefferson Court Projects were built across town for white families. Public housing was sponsored by the federal government to provide reasonably priced housing for working-class people. President Roosevelt started the program in 1937 to address the housing crisis brought on by the Great Depression, when many people lost their homes and could not find decent, affordable places to live. The government provided local authorities with loans to construct

Cleveland Court Projects. The Parks family lived in #634.

low-rent housing, and the resulting housing projects based
rent prices on residents' income. The Parkses moved into
Apartment 634 at the Cleveland Court apartments some-
time in 1942 or 1943.

By 1947, Rosa Parks's political reputation had grown.
She was chosen to serve on the executive committee for
the Alabama conference of the NAACP, which encouraged
E. D. Nixon to run for head of the state's organization to
bring his political vision to even more Alabamians. He
ran, won, and served in the position from 1947 to 1949.

Though Parks usually shied away from public speaking, she overcame her reluctance to give a fiery speech
at the state convention, urging members not to be complacent. She spoke out against the mistreatment of Black
women in the South and criticized those "feeling proud

of their home or the South when Negroes every day are being molested and maltreated. No one should feel proud of a place where Negroes are intimidated." Her speech was met with thunderous applause—and Parks was subsequently elected the first secretary of the Alabama conference of the NAACP.

She traveled around Alabama, recording information about the problems Black people faced across the state. "Rosa will talk to you," Raymond said as she took down dozens of testimonies of the brutality and sexual violence white people used to terrorize the Black community. Parks urged the people she spoke with to file complaints detailing this violence with the US Department of Justice. The NAACP wanted to prove a pattern of violence against Black people and demonstrate the lack of attention by law enforcement. Rosa's compassion and ability to see what was needed matched her larger vision that injustice did not have to be a way of life. Many people were willing to talk to her.

But many who shared their stories with her were also worried that they'd be punished if they filed a formal complaint. They worried about retaliation from their white neighbors or the local authorities, and fearing for their lives and those of their loved ones, they refused to sign an affidavit, or official document, about what had happened to them.

Parks was also putting herself in great danger by traveling to compile these testimonies. Shy as she was, Rosa proved through her actions that she wasn't afraid to face the danger of fighting for what she believed in. She and Nixon also sent letters supporting antilynching legislation to the federal government.

One case that gutted them was the rape of Gertrude Perkins by two Montgomery police officers in 1949. Parks and Nixon were outraged. At first, the police commissioner pursued charges against the officers. But then the mayor blamed the incident on the NAACP, and the grand jury dismissed the charges against the officers. Police records were changed to protect the officers who had raped Perkins. Parks felt herself growing bitter and depressed. Over and over, the law didn't protect Black people—and Black women in particular. And their efforts to expose the problem seemed to be at a standstill. "People blamed the NAACP for not winning cases," she wrote, "when they did not support it and give [it] strength enough."

Meanwhile, Raymond was becoming increasingly angry at how many Black people were unwilling to stand up for themselves. Rosa was disappointed, but she understood the pressure people felt. Violence was always a threat, but so was economic retaliation, meaning people could lose their jobs if they spoke up. Plus, many Black people felt hopeless; they thought protesting injustice was pointless because they felt they would never be treated as equals with white people.

Rosa Parks's writing on how Black rebels were demonized.

Racial justice activism in the 1940s was an extremely difficult, regularly demoralizing, and often terrifying activity. Most people shied away. There was no indication that you would see change in your lifetime, and it meant fighting against the very fear and hopelessness that white supremacy encouraged (and the retaliation that often accompanied it). Parks knew that many Black people thought she and other activists, like Nixon and Carr, were foolish or dangerous. "Such a good job of brain washing was done on the Negro," Parks wrote, "that a militant Negro was almost a freak of nature to them, many times ridiculed by others of his own group."

But for Rosa Parks, as it had been since she was a kid, it was imperative to dissent, to "say you didn't like it." And so this group of activists was precious to her. They sustained her spirits, as did her mother and Raymond, whom she could talk to about her growing frustrations with the violence of white resistance and lack of action from many Black people.

So did watching baseball. Something exciting happened in 1947. Jackie Robinson joined the Brooklyn Dodgers and became the first Black person to play major league baseball. Mrs. Parks had always loved baseball and had long followed the Negro Leagues (the baseball leagues created so great Black players could play). She listened to as many games on the radio as she could, and she kept track of Robinson's career carefully.

■ ■ ■

Times were tough in Montgomery. Her own brother had decided to leave and moved to Detroit, Michigan, in

Rosa's brother, Sylvester McCauley

1946. He'd served in the 1318th Medical Detachment Engineering Services Regiment during World War II. When he returned to Montgomery after the war, despite his courageous service to his country, he was treated as an "uppity Negro." He couldn't find work and wasn't able to register to vote. Rosa said that returning Black veterans "were treated with even more disrespect, especially if they were in uniform. Whites felt things should remain as they had always been and that Black veterans were getting too sassy. My brother was one who could not take that kind of treatment anymore." Many veterans found it so unbearable that some moved, as Sylvester did—as part of what was called the Great Migration, from the South to other parts of the country—searching for a better place to live. Others became leaders of the civil rights struggle in the South in the following decades.

Sylvester left Montgomery for Detroit in 1946 and never returned. He and his wife, Daisy, eventually had thirteen children. When they first moved to Detroit to find work, they left their two children at the time, Mary and Sylvester Jr., to stay with Rosa, Raymond, and Rosa's mother, Leona, who lived with the Parkses. A year or so later, once Sylvester found work on a Chrysler auto assembly line, Daisy returned to Alabama to get the two children; they had grown close to Rosa, so it was a difficult separation.

Though Detroit was a less hostile place than Montgomery to lay down roots, the city was plagued with rampant segregation and job discrimination. Sylvester struggled for several years just to feed his family. Rosa wondered if there might be a place for her in Detroit too. In 1948, she went to visit her brother in Detroit. As a Black woman, her job prospects in Montgomery were limited, and though Detroit had its problems, she thought the Northern city might provide her more opportunities. A friend from the NAACP wrote her at her brother's, saying that E. D. Nixon was depressed over her departure and complained about how most Black Montgomerians were unwilling to take action in the face of repeated injustice: "The Negroes here are slipping and sliding. I guess it would take an atom bomb to jar them out of their complacency and into action." Rosa and her group of friends had begun to feel like there would never be a mass movement in Montgomery.

Whether Rosa could not find work in Detroit or because she and Raymond were not ready to leave their home in Alabama is unclear, but Rosa did return to Montgomery and to her political activities with the NAACP. And Sylvester and his family continued to struggle in Detroit. One letter he wrote to them read, "We are just existing on what we can get. . . . I wish I could come home. I am very tired of living like this."

In 1949, Rosa's mother got sick, and Rosa cut back on her NAACP work to care for her. However, with Parks away from the branch, the national office began to question Nixon's leadership more and more, and quietly plotted to replace him with a more traditional—that is, less political—middle-class leader. That November, Nixon lost the state conference presidency to a Birmingham-based insurance agent named W. C. Patton. The next year,

Nixon also lost his branch presidency—to another insurance agent, named Robert Matthews. The former chapter leader still participated in some areas of NAACP work, but Nixon had grown disillusioned with the branch's lack of action in many areas. He was still running the Brotherhood of Sleeping Car Porters chapter and leading the Progressive Democratic Association, a local group interested in Democratic Party politics that were less racist than those found in the South. Parks continued to help him with both.

Rosa Parks returned to a more active role and to her position as NAACP branch secretary in 1952. E. D. Nixon wasn't very pleased, given the branch's return to middle-class leadership. One of the issues that continued to weigh on her was the way the criminal justice system operated for Black people. Black women in particular were often unprotected from the sexual violence and brutality of white people, while the justice system was quick to punish Black men, often framing them for false crimes when they "got out of their place."

It was hard to find lawyers who would agree to work on these cases. However, Parks was excited when a former classmate from Miss White's school returned to Montgomery and set up a legal practice. Mahalia Dickerson had earned a degree from Fisk University in Nashville, Tennessee, and then attended law school at Howard University in Washington, DC. When she graduated and moved back home, she became the first Black female lawyer in the state of Alabama. She worked with Parks on the cases of several Black prisoners at Kilby Prison, but Parks said her old classmate "did not receive the support she needed from the African-American community." So Dickerson left.

Parks was haunted by the case of one particular young man: sixteen-year-old Jeremiah Reeves. Popular at his high school, Reeves was a jazz drummer and delivered groceries after school for work. He'd also started seeing a young white woman. When neighbors found out about their secret relationship, the young woman got scared about the reputation she'd get for being with a Black man, so she accused Reeves of rape. The police arrested him, brought him to jail, and forced him to sit in the electric chair until they coerced a confession out of him—a confession he later took back.

Rosa Parks and others fought for years to try to prevent Reeves's execution. His lawyers managed to get the Supreme Court to overturn the conviction because the jury had been all-white. But the struggle wasn't over yet, as *another* all-white jury convicted Reeves for a second time. The young man wrote poems in prison while awaiting his fate, which Rosa tried to get published. She saved his poems for decades. In the end, his supporters were unsuccessful. The conviction was not overturned, and the State of Alabama electrocuted Jeremiah Reeves on March 28, 1958. He was twenty-two years old.

Parks kept working for change, but she also grew increasingly discouraged by cases like Reeves's. "It was hard to keep going," she said, "when all our efforts seemed in vain."

# CHAPTER SIX

# THE NAACP YOUTH COUNCIL GETS A FRESH START

Since she'd begun working with the NAACP, Rosa Parks understood that young people were the key to carrying forward the organization's hard work. She often felt they were more willing to directly challenge discrimination than many of her adult peers. So she and Johnnie Carr formed a youth council for the branch, encouraging its members to participate in fighting racial injustice.

In December 1947, she took a group of young people to see the Freedom Train, a national exhibit that was touring the country. The train, painted red, white, and blue, showcased the United States' founding documents, displaying original copies of the Declaration of Independence, the Constitution, and the Bill of Rights. The exhibit came with a requirement that applied to every city it visited: it was open to all, regardless of their race. The crowds would not be segregated, meaning white and Black people would be free to mingle with one another.

This rule did not sit well with many white people, who tried to stop the exhibit from coming to their cities. In fact, the train bypassed Birmingham and Memphis altogether because city leaders refused to agree to the terms. But Rosa Parks and her colleagues ensured the local Freedom Train committee in Montgomery included Black people and that all visitors would enter on a first-come, first-served basis.

This was the first time the Parks family received hateful phone calls and death threats as a result of her activism. But she was adamant that the young Black people in Montgomery recognize they had rights and feel entitled to the same opportunities as white people, so she escorted them to the exhibit. Despite her efforts, though, the Youth Council's involvement faded and eventually ended.

Over the years, as Mrs. Parks worried that she might not see change in her lifetime, she once again focused her energy on cultivating the leadership of young people. In 1954, she decided to revive Montgomery's NAACP Youth Council. She was discouraged by the "complacency" of many of her peers, and she admired the fighting spirit of young people. Parks and her husband never had children of their own, but she loved kids, and throughout her life, she was energized by the determination of the youth around her.

The Youth Council met most Sundays at the Parkses' Cleveland Court apartment. But when they hosted speakers, they moved across the street to Trinity Lutheran, a Black church run by a white pastor named Robert Graetz. Being part of the Youth Council, which included young people ages twelve to twenty, wasn't always a popular choice; most parents didn't want their children affiliated with the NAACP. "At that time, the NAACP was considered far too militant, or too radical, or too dangerous," Parks said.

Many young people were warned by their parents and teachers not to get involved in civil rights. "There was this very popular phrase: 'In order to stay out of trouble you have to stay in your place,'" she explained. "But when you stayed in your place, you were still insulted and mistreated if they saw fit to do so." Mrs. Parks wanted to show these young people a different way forward.

With her small group of young people, she helped them see past the oppression they experienced every day, showing them the inequality in Montgomery was not right nor was it their destiny. She helped them realize they could be forces for change. During the meetings, she stressed the importance of listening, studying, and neatness and encouraged them to aim high, providing information on college options and scholarships.

The Youth Council traveled across the state, where they attended meetings, provided citizenship education, and helped adults prepare for the voter registration test. Student leader Doris Crenshaw said, "People were fearful of registering to vote. So we encouraged them to go down [to the voter registration office], to not be afraid."

Parks enjoyed how focused the Youth Council members were, which was different from the adult NAACP members, who often argued over the processes before they did any work. The young people "started right in to write letters to Washington [DC, over antilynching legislation]. . . . They didn't spend a lot of time arguing over motions." Parks urged them to take stronger stands against segregation, and when she took them downtown, they "always drank from the white water fountain."

The Youth Council decided to hold a protest over the segregation of public libraries. Black people were only allowed to use the "colored branch" instead of the main downtown branch, which held a wider selection of books. The teenagers of the Youth Council protested by visiting the downtown location and requesting to be served. "They did this again and again," Parks said, though they were unsuccessful in reversing the segregation. But their spirit of determination grew.

White supremacy "walks us on a tightrope from birth," so Mrs. Parks understood the "major mental acrobatic feat" it took to survive as a young Black person. She worried about the damaging effects segregation had on children and stressed the hardships that came with enduring racism in America and the constant pressure to conform or give up entirely. She tried to build for her Youth Council a way to imagine beyond the tightrope.

Racism seemed like a never-ending battle, and she was worn down by fighting the system of injustice, saying there is "just so much hurt, disappointment, and oppression one can take. . . . The line between reason and madness grows thinner."

Mrs. Parks had seen the punishments doled out to Black rebels; she and Raymond knew people who'd been shot at or murdered, fired from their jobs, or forced out of the town where they made their home. Feeling like "puppets on the string in the white man's hand," Rosa

I want to feel the nearness of something secure. It is such a lonely, lost feeling that I am cut off from life. I am nothing, I belong nowhere and to no one.

There is just so much hurt, disappointment and oppression one can take. The bubble of life grows larger. The line between reason and madness grows thinner. The reopening of old wounds are unbearably painful.

Parks found the constant struggle to negotiate white supremacy lonely and difficult.

lamented how "we perform to their satisfaction or suffer the consequence if we get out of line."

Yet, she didn't want the young people she worked with to suffer from this kind of mental conditioning. So she began to show them how to refuse to perform.

# CHAPTER SEVEN

# RESISTANCE + ANGER = SEEDS OF CHANGE

The problem of segregation, which Rosa Parks called "a complete and solid pattern as a way of life," was especially apparent when it came to the bus system in Montgomery. White people sat in the front, while Black people were supposed to sit in the back. Black riders were allowed to sit in the middle of the bus, but they could be forced to move "on the whim of a driver" if a white rider was standing. There were exceptions to these rules, as they primarily existed to ensure the "wealth and comfort" of white people. For example, a Black woman working as a nanny for white children was allowed to sit at the front of the bus.

The bus was one of the places where segregation's power was felt most immediately. Black people could actively be treated differently—could be told to get up, in front of others, which was even more humiliating. "You died a little each time you found yourself face to face with this kind of discrimination," Parks explained.

The bus company only hired white people as drivers. And bus drivers had police powers and carried guns. Some of them didn't even like Black passengers walking next to the white riders when they boarded the bus, so the drivers would force them to pay at the front and then exit the bus and reboard through the back door. And sometimes these drivers would drive away before the passenger had a chance to reboard, taking their money and leaving them stranded.

Not all bus drivers treated Black riders so poorly, said Rosalyn Oliver King and Doris Crenshaw, who were members of the NAACP Youth Council. Some allowed Black passengers to sit in the front seats while they drove through the Black parts of town. But that kindness usually evaporated as soon as they entered a white neighborhood; most drivers would make the passengers move to the back. And even the kindest bus drivers were no match for a system of segregation.

Jo Ann Robinson, head of the Women's Political Council, a middle-class Black women's organization in Montgomery, remembered the demeaning terms bus drivers would often use to address Black women, referring to them as animals and using ethnic slurs. Dr. Martin Luther King Jr. highlighted this abuse, adding that bus drivers said things like "Get back, you ugly Black apes" and "I'm gonna show you n——rs that we got laws in Alabama."

Rosa and Raymond Parks avoided the bus when they could. But it was often impossible as a working-class person who worked downtown and didn't have a car. Raymond had a car when he and Rosa first got married,

Raymond Parks, second from left, in front of
Atlas Barber Shop, where he worked for two decades.

but they hit hard times and couldn't afford it. Then, in
1952, Raymond lost his job of twenty years at Atlas
Barber Shop, so their economic situation grew even more
uncertain.

Rosa wasn't the first in her family to speak up against
mistreatment on the bus. "Protest must be in my blood,"
Rosa said. Her mother, Leona, had resisted segregation
on the bus when Rosa was a teenager. The bus driver
approached Leona, who was sitting at the back next to
a white man, and told her that she had to move or he'd
throw her off. Leona "stood up, very politely smiled in
his face, and said, 'You won't do that.'" A Black man
nearby said, "If he touches her, I'm hanging my knife in
his throat." Rosa herself was ready to fight off the driver

with her bare hands if need be. But he didn't touch her mother and returned to the front.

Although Rosa's bus resistance became part of civil rights history, challenging segregation "was just a regular thing with me and not just that day." Parks stood up to bus driver James Blake for the first time in 1943. Blake was a driver who made Black passengers pay up front, get off the bus, and reboard in the back. Parks refused. And when she didn't move, Blake grabbed her sleeve and tried to push her off the bus. Then Parks purposefully dropped her purse and sat down on the front seat to retrieve it, practically daring him to respond. It seemed as if he was going to hit her. "I will get off," she told him. "You better not touch me." She exited the bus and did not get back on.

After this incident, Parks tried to avoid Blake's bus. But she was thrown off other buses by other drivers for refusing to reboard in the back after she'd paid. Some drivers told her not to ride if she was "too important . . . to go to the back and get on." And some recognized her because of her resistance. "It seemed to annoy and sometimes anger the bus drivers," she said. One particular driver would shut the bus door as fast as he could and drive away if he saw her standing alone on the curb.

Rosa Parks wasn't the first Black person in Montgomery to be arrested for refusing to submit to bus segregation. In the decade before her famous arrest, a small trickle of Black riders also took a stand, in line with the increase of Black resistance during World War II.

A Black woman named Viola White was arrested in 1944 for refusing to move and decided to pursue her case in court. The police retaliated by raping her sixteen-year-old daughter, who had the presence of mind to memorize the cop's license plate and report the crime. The officer was never punished. Viola White's court case went on for years, as the state used legal maneuvers to tie it up and not let it come up on appeal. White died before it was resolved.

In 1946, another Black woman, Geneva Johnson, was arrested, this time for "talking back" to a bus driver—and for not having the correct change. Indeed, Black people were often thrown off the bus for "making noise."

A few years later, Mary Wingfield was arrested for sitting in seats reserved for white people, and in 1949, two New Jersey residents, Edwin and Marshall Johnson, refused to give up their seats and were arrested. They were teenagers.

In 1950, a Black veteran named Hilliard Brooks refused to get off the bus and reboard from the back, just as Parks had. Brooks argued with the bus driver, which passenger Mattie Johnson witnessed. She said, "When you're waitin' on something awful to happen, you feel it more than any other time. It feels like it's pressing down on you, getting tighter and tighter around you, cuttin' you off from everything else."

The police were called, and when Officer M. E. Mills boarded the bus, he hit Brooks with his club. Brooks managed to get free and tried to exit the bus, but the police officer shot Brooks—who ended up dying from his wounds. The murder haunted Mattie Johnson, who never rode the bus again. Officer Mills was never punished for his crime, as the murder was ruled justifiable because Mills said that Hilliard Brooks had "resisted arrest."

The NAACP worked on many of these cases, with Rosa Parks by E. D. Nixon's side, and she knew a number of the people involved. The Brooks family were Rosa's neighbors at Cleveland Court. So not only did Parks know how some people had resisted bus segregation, but she also understood the horrible consequences many suffered for it.

May 1954 was a turning point in the fight against segregation: the US Supreme Court found school segregation unconstitutional in *Brown v. Board of Education*, effectively overturning the 1896 case of *Plessy v. Ferguson*, which had decided that segregated facilities were legal so long as they were "separate but equal." In this new ruling, the court said that "separate educational facilities are inherently unequal" and affirmed education as "a right that must be made available to all on equal terms." *Brown* was a landmark decision, as Black children had not received the same educational opportunities as white children.

The ruling specifically applied to schools, but many people saw it as the beginning of the end of other forms of segregation, because *Brown* could be used to challenge other areas of the law. People began to contemplate bringing a legal case against bus segregation. But they needed a good case—someone the community would rally around.

The Women's Political Council (WPC), a group of middle-class Black women in Montgomery, was excited by the *Brown v. Board of Education* decision. Founded in 1949 by Mary Fair Burks, an Alabama State College professor—and Rosa's former classmate—the WPC had become increasingly vocal against bus segregation. (Parks was not a member of the WPC, likely because of class and education divides within the Black community.) Jo Ann Robinson, who'd become president of the organization in 1952 and was also a professor at Alabama State, had been degraded by a driver just three years earlier, in 1949. She'd been kicked off a near-empty bus for sitting too close to the front. "Tears blinded my vision," Robinson remembered. "Waves of humiliation inundated me; and I thanked God that none of my students was on that bus to witness the tragic experience. I could have died from embarrassment."

Robinson, who'd been afraid the driver was going to hit her, had fled the bus immediately. She was so traumatized by the experience that she didn't even talk to her close friends about it. But that moment was the fuel she and the WPC needed to keep demanding change on the Montgomery buses. Not long after the *Brown* decision, Robinson wrote to the mayor of Montgomery on behalf of the Women's Political Council and threatened a bus boycott if the segregation did not stop.

The pressure was on.

# CHAPTER EIGHT

# CLAUDETTE COLVIN SITS DOWN (AND RISES UP)

Hope was in the air as 1955 began. After the Supreme Court's decision in the *Brown* case, Montgomery residents believed that bus segregation could also soon be ruled unconstitutional.

But not everyone was happy about the decision. Many white people in both the South *and* the North were upset, and Southern states began to work together to fight the federal ruling. The next year, in 1956, eighty-two congressmen and nineteen senators from the South introduced the Southern Manifesto, which called *Brown* an abuse of judicial power over states' rights. Some Northerners resisted the decision, too, but they didn't want to be lumped together with the South, so many simply acted as if the ruling did not apply to them and their schools.

Rosa Parks and E. D. Nixon were thrilled about the *Brown* decision. "You can't imagine the rejoicing among black people," Parks said, with the "possibility of not having to continue as we had" in Montgomery's firmly segregated school system. However, when Nixon and several others escorted twenty-three Black children to the newly built all-white William Harrison School, Nixon said, the school officials "wouldn't let them stay there. They run them out, and they run me out, too."

At a meeting of the Montgomery branch of the NAACP, members decided to directly pressure the local school board and began to seek out signatures for a petition pushing for desegregation. A few Black parents signed the petition, and the NAACP branch presented the plan to the board of education at the beginning of the school year in 1954. The board responded by publishing the names and addresses of all the people who had signed, hoping to intimidate them into backing down.

It worked. The Black parents were unwilling to pursue the case further and take the city to court for fear of even more retaliation and hostility. Parks grew very discouraged.

Nixon didn't think that the Montgomery NAACP branch had done enough to try to overturn segregation, so he continued to pressure the chapter and the national NAACP to increase their efforts in working toward school desegregation. The Montgomery Board of Education wouldn't budge. This wasn't unique. Most school districts around the country were ignoring the Supreme Court's decision and demonizing anyone who dared to speak up about desegregation.

Rosa thought the situation was "hopeless" and grew depressed by the "apathy on the part of our people" to insist the Supreme Court's decision be followed.

Claudette Colvin

A new person soon joined the fight for desegregation. On March 2, 1955, fifteen-year-old Claudette Colvin was riding home from school with several of her classmates. The white section of the bus filled up, and a white woman was left to stand. Bus driver Robert Cleere ordered Colvin to move.

The petite Colvin refused.

So Cleere had the teenager arrested.

Claudette Colvin hadn't forgotten what happened to Jeremiah Reeves, the young man who'd been falsely accused and wrongfully convicted, and was sitting on death row. Reeves had attended Colvin's high school, and her political consciousness began to increase after his arrest. Colvin said his case was

the turning point of my life. That was when I and a lot of other students really started thinking about prejudice and racism. . . . When a white man raped a Black girl—something that happened all the time—it was just his word against hers, and no one would ever believe her. The white man always got off. But now they were going to hold Jeremiah for years as a minor just so they could legally execute him when he came of age. That changed me. . . . I stayed angry for a long time.

Colvin had been studying Black history and the US Constitution at the segregated Booker T. Washington

High School in Montgomery—and she knew she had rights. This knowledge helped her take a stand when the driver asked her to move.

When she didn't get up, the driver called out to her again: "Why are you still sittin' there?" Colvin recalled, "A white rider yelled from the front, 'You got to get up!'"

Thirteen students sat on the bus that day, most of them Colvin's classmates. A girl named Margaret Johnson called back, "She ain't got to do nothin' but stay Black and die!"

The bus driver called the police, but Colvin didn't back down. She was tired of standing for white people every day. When law enforcement showed up, the bus driver told them, "I've had trouble with that 'thing' before."

"He called me a thing," Colvin said.

Though she began to cry, she held strong and resisted the demands that she get up. "It's my constitutional right to sit here as much as that lady," Colvin insisted.

The police didn't care that she was a small fifteen-year-old girl. They roughly lifted her out of the seat and slapped handcuffs on her. Colvin went limp, and they dragged her from the bus, continuing to handle her roughly. She struggled against them, scratching at the officers as they put her in their police car.

In the patrol car, they mocked her, making rude comments about her body, and Colvin was scared they would sexually assault her. She tried to cover her lap and think of other things to get her mind off the arrest: "I recited Edgar Allan Poe, 'Annabel Lee,' the characters in *Midsummer Night's Dream*, the Lord's Prayer, and the 23rd Psalm." When they arrived at the station, more officers there said insulting things to her. They booked her on three charges: disturbing the peace, assaulting an officer, and violating the segregation law.

The Black community was outraged, and Rosa Parks and her friends started a fundraising campaign for Colvin's case. Soon, more than one hundred letters and donations began streaming into Parks's apartment to support the cause. In the meantime, Parks encouraged Colvin to become an active member of Montgomery's NAACP Youth Council.

Colvin remembered meeting Rosa Parks for the first time: "She said, 'You're Claudette Colvin? Oh my god. I was lookin' for some big old burly overgrown teenager who sassed white people out. . . . But no, they pulled a little girl off the bus.'"

Twenty-four-year-old Fred Gray agreed to be Colvin's attorney. The young lawyer had returned to Montgomery after earning a law degree at Case Western Reserve University School of Law in Ohio in 1954. Gray had grown up in Alabama. But the state wouldn't let Black people attend its own state law school and didn't want to invest in a separate law school for Black people, so it paid the tuition to send Black students out of state to study.

Gray attended law school because he was "determined to destroy everything segregated I could find." When he came back to Montgomery, he was one of only two Black lawyers in the city, and one of only twelve in the entire state. He began working with the local NAACP, and Rosa Parks quickly took him under her wing, delighted to have a Black lawyer in Montgomery who was committed to change.

"We became very good friends," Gray said. Parks would often visit his office during her lunch break, helping him get his law practice off the ground and encouraging him to pursue civil rights issues. "She gave me the feeling that I was the Moses that God had sent Pharaoh and commanded him to 'let my people go.'"

Put On Indefinite Probation

## Negro Girl Found Guilty Of Segregation Violation

*Alabama Journal*, March 19, 1955

Gray went to Colvin's house to make clear the risk she was taking in pursuing her case. He told the teenager that her name would be in the newspaper, which could harm her and her family—both physically and financially. Colvin insisted that she wanted to go forward with the case.

To calm the increasing outrage from the Black community about Colvin's arrest, the City of Montgomery and the bus company promised to make changes. At one meeting, a group of Black leaders presented them with a petition asking for more respectful treatment on the bus. But Parks did not join them. "I had decided I would not go anywhere with a piece of paper in my hand asking white folks for any favors," she said. According to Parks, the Black community had to deal with many useless meetings and "some vague promises and . . . nothing was ever done" about the bus segregation issue.

Colvin's case was heard on May 6, 1955. The judge, perhaps strategically, dropped two of the charges, for disturbing the peace and disobeying segregation. That made it more difficult to launch a direct challenge to the segregation law. However, the judge did find Colvin guilty of assaulting the officers who'd arrested her, which Virginia Durr wrote a friend was "cowardly," as this was "THREE HUGE POLICEMEN against one little, scrawny fifteen-year-old colored girl."

After her court appearance, Colvin stopped straightening her hair to protest yet another aspect of white supremacy. "By wearing it natural," she said, "I was saying, 'I think I'm as pretty as you are.'" Colvin decided she wouldn't straighten her hair until the courts "straighten out this mess . . . until we [get] some justice." Many people at the time looked down upon wearing Black hair natural, and a number of her classmates teased Colvin about her hair and her arrest. "Everyone blamed her rather than the people who did those things to her," one classmate recalled. "We should have been rallying around her and being proud of what she had done, but instead we ridiculed her."

The judge had made it harder to pursue the case by dropping the segregation charge. And Colvin's supporters grew wobbly because many community leaders didn't believe she was the right kind of plaintiff. Colvin was young, poor, and dark-skinned. And because of her young age, some Black leaders, including E. D. Nixon, didn't have confidence that she would present herself well in court. He and other leaders saw Colvin as "uncontrollable" and "emotional," and they didn't feel she was the right person for a test case. And so they decided not to pursue her case and began to distance themselves from the young woman.

Jo Ann Robinson of the Women's Political Council disagreed with their view, as did Colvin's lawyer, Fred Gray. Rosa Parks may have disagreed, too, but it's unclear if she ever told Nixon. Later that summer, Parks said, "I wanted our leaders there to organize and be strong enough to back up and support any young person who

quickly learned that Parks had been arrested on a charge of violating segregation law.

Nixon and the Durrs headed down to the station to bail her out. The Durrs didn't have any money, and Nixon posted bail for Rosa, but he still wanted the white couple to go with him to ensure the police released Parks after taking his money. Around nine thirty that evening, Parks walked out of jail to greet her friends. Virginia Durr was surprised by how calm she seemed. As they were leaving, Raymond appeared with a bail bondsman, so Rosa rode home with her husband.

Everyone went back to the Parkses' apartment to talk about what they should do next. They drank coffee and went over all the options until around eleven o'clock that evening. Clifford Durr thought he could get the charges dismissed if Rosa wanted, as there had not been an open seat on the bus for her to move to. Montgomery had a law, although typically not enforced, that said a Black person could not be asked to move if there were no open seats in the back they could move to.

Once Nixon realized that Parks hadn't been harmed, he was somewhat delighted by the arrest. *This* was the opportunity the activists had been waiting for to launch a legal attack on segregation. Nixon talked extensively about the possibility of a legal challenge: "It'll be a long, hard struggle. . . . It won't cost you and Mr. Parks anything but time and misery. But I think it will be worth all the time and misery." Rosa knew she would never ride a segregated bus again, but she had to consider whether she wanted to make a public case and step into the line of attack.

Raymond did not support the idea at first. He was terrified for his wife's safety and worried she might be killed if she pursued the case. He also worried the community might not stand behind in the long term, which is what had happened with Claudette Colvin.

After their visitors left, Raymond, Rosa, and her mother kept talking. In the end, both Leona and Raymond supported Rosa's decision to move forward with the case. "They were against segregation and were willing to fight it," she said.

So, late that evening, Rosa Parks called Fred Gray and asked him to represent her in a legal case against segregation. Gray agreed and said that, from that moment, "my days of having little to do in my fledgling law practice were over."

After he got off the phone with his new client, Gray called Jo Ann Robinson to let her know Parks's decision to pursue a case. Over that evening, the word of Parks's arrest had rippled through Montgomery's Black community, but, Robinson said, people seemed paralyzed. "There was fear, discontent, and uncertainty. Everyone seemed to wait for someone to *do* something, but nobody made a move."

Robinson decided to do something. She called the Women's Political Council leadership; it was these women who decided—late that night—to call for a one-day bus boycott on Monday, the day Parks was scheduled to appear in court.

A Black woman being out alone in the dead of night was quite dangerous in Montgomery, but Robinson still headed to Alabama State College, where she worked, to begin planning. With the help of two students and a colleague who let her use the mimeograph machine to make copies, Robinson stayed up till the next morning printing leaflets announcing the boycott:

This is for Monday, December 5, 1955

Another Negro woman has been arrested and thrown into jail because she refused to get up out of her seat on the bus for a white person to sit down.

It is the second time since the Claudette Colbert case that a Negro woman has been arrested for the same thing This has to be stopped.

Negroes have rights, too, for if Negroes did not ride the buses, they could not operate. Three-fourths of the riders are Negroes, yet we are arrested, or have to stand over empty seats. If we do not do something to stop these arrests, they will continue. The next time it may be you, or your daughter, or mother.

This woman's case will come up on Monday. We are, therefore, asking every Negro to stay off the buses Monday in protest of the arrest and trial. Don't ride the buses to work, to town, to school, or anywhere on Monday.

You can afford to stay out of school for one day if you have no other way to go except by bus.
You can also afford to stay out of town for one day. If you work, take a cab, or walk. But please, children and grown-ups, don't ride the bus at all on Monday. Please stay off of all buses

The WPC leaflet made clear that Parks's arrest was not an isolated incident. An accumulation of injustice from Claudette Colvin to Mary Louise Smith to now Rosa Parks had led them here. Black Montgomerians had reached their breaking point, and it was time to take action.

Part of the reason people rallied behind Rosa Parks was that she was a forty-two-year-old married woman who was active in her church and the community. To them, she presented the right image.

Also, the community trusted her, given her longtime work as an activist. They knew she was brave and rightly believed she wouldn't flinch under the intimidation inflicted on people who challenged segregation.

Parks was solidly working class, but the way she presented herself also appealed to the Black middle class.

People saw themselves in her—and they felt that if this could happen to her, it could happen to them. According to WPC founder Mary Fair Burks, Parks "possessed sterling qualities" that Black middle-class leaders "were forced to admire in spite of their usual indifference."

As the community began to react following the arrest, Colvin experienced a rush of feelings: "I was glad an adult had finally stood up to the system, but I felt left out. I was thinking, Hey, I did that months ago and everybody dropped me. . . . But on the other hand, having been with Rosa at the NAACP meetings, I thought, Well, maybe she's the right person—she's strong, and adults won't listen to me anyway."

Colvin's arrest had certainly laid the foundation for the anger that led to the boycott. According to Black teacher Sarah Coleman, part of the widespread outrage upon Parks's arrest stemmed from broken promises following Colvin's case: "When that high school girl was arrested last spring . . . the bus company promised us they would do something, and in six months they never did anything."

For Parks and many Black people in Montgomery, the protest was much bigger than a bus seat. This was about challenging the discriminatory power structure, disrespectful treatment, and unequal distribution of goods, jobs, and resources that segregation enabled. As Parks told an interviewer in the mid-1960s, "I have never been what you would call just an integrationist. . . . Even when there was segregation, there was plenty of integration in the South, but it was for the benefit and convenience of the white person, not us. "So, it is not just integration."

# CHAPTER TWELVE

# A BOYCOTT BLOSSOMS

The night Rosa Parks was arrested, Jo Ann Robinson and her students copied 52,500 leaflets. At around 3:00 a.m., Robinson phoned E. D. Nixon to let him know of their plans for a boycott on Monday.

But she did not call Parks. In fact, she later wrote in her autobiography that she felt she didn't need to. This may have stemmed from the educational and class differences between Robinson, a college professor, and working-class Parks, who'd never been able to attend college. It's possible Robinson didn't see Parks as someone whose input was needed in the planning of the boycott, and she likely didn't know the full extent of Parks's long history of activism. Plus, as the leaflet made clear, the boycott wasn't about a single incident but a pattern of injustice.

From 4:00 a.m. to 7:00 a.m. that Friday morning, Robinson and her students mapped out distribution routes, then met with nearly twenty women from the Women's Political Council, who spread out across the city, leaving leaflets anywhere they would be seen and appreciated: barbershops, stores, bars, factories, and churches.

Nixon rose early that Friday morning too; he was headed out of town for his Pullman train job, and he wanted to get Montgomery's more political ministers on board for the Monday boycott. His first call was to Reverend Ralph Abernathy. The twenty-nine-year-old Abernathy was one of the few politically active ministers in town and a member of the NAACP. Then, at around six in the morning, Nixon phoned Martin Luther King Jr. The young reverend hesitated when Nixon asked to use his church for a meeting that evening. His newborn baby, Yolanda, was only three weeks old, and he wasn't sure he could commit, given his and his wife Coretta's new family responsibilities. "Let me think about it a while and call me back," he told Nixon.

Looking back on that Friday morning, it's important to recognize that there was nothing destined about King's leadership, no lightning bolt that showed him what to do. He had no idea the tremendous role he would play in the months and years ahead. Like everyone else, he had to make difficult decision after difficult decision, to take action without a road map of where it could lead. Similar to Mrs. Parks, part of King's genius was the ability to step forward without a clear path ahead. This was the start of King's growing leadership, and by the end of the boycott, he had gained national notice. But there was nothing easy or obvious about the role he would come to play.

A few hours later, Nixon called King back, and the young minister said the group could meet at his church.

Nixon, Abernathy, and King worked through the morning to find other ministers to attend that evening.

Friday morning, the first thing Rosa Parks did was call the brother of the woman who'd been in the cell with her to let him know what was happening to his sister.

She wasn't going to ride the bus, so she took a cab to work instead. Her coworkers were surprised to see her. "You don't think that going to jail is going to keep me home, do you?" she joked. But she didn't know a boycott had been called in her name until she went to Fred Gray's office for lunch. She was shocked to see the leaflets and hear about the plans for the Monday boycott. When Nixon called to tell her about the meeting at Dexter Avenue Baptist Church that evening, she asked what it was for. "You know—about your being arrested," he replied.

Parks said she would be there.

Before he left on his Pullman trip, Nixon had to talk to one more person: a young white reporter for the *Montgomery Advertiser*. Joe Azbell was no supporter of Black civil rights and, in fact, would go on to oppose the boycott throughout its run. But Nixon knew Azbell would be interested in the "scoop," so he gave the reporter a leaflet. Azbell was interested all right—so interested that he published a front-page story in the *Montgomery Advertiser* that Sunday, reprinting the entire leaflet and ensuring that many Black people who hadn't seen the leaflet were now aware of the boycott.

Nixon laughed at how "panicky white folks" gave the impending protest so much exposure: "We couldn't have paid for the free publicity the white folks gave our boycott." Two local television stations and four radio stations also picked up the news. The protest was officially a public event.

Later that day, Parks spoke with Reverend Robert Graetz, whose church, Trinity Lutheran, was across the street from Cleveland Court and where she sometimes had NAACP Youth Council meetings. Graetz had become pastor of the Black church that year and was committed to racial equality. He and his wife, Jean, who were both white, were not respected by other white people in Montgomery for the way they mingled with the Black community. In addition to pastoring a Black congregation, Graetz and his wife sat in the Black section at the movie theater. White people shunned them when they were out shopping.

Graetz had heard about Rosa's arrest and the plans for the boycott, but as a white man, he couldn't get much information. So he called Parks, one of his closest Black acquaintances, and said, "I just heard that someone was arrested on one of the buses Thursday."

"That's right, Pastor Graetz," Parks replied.

"And that we're supposed to boycott the buses on Monday to protest," he said.

"That's right, Pastor Graetz."

"Do you know anything about it?"

"Yes, Pastor Graetz."

"Do you know who was arrested?"

"Yes, Pastor Graetz."

"Well, who was it?"

Parks let the silence grow between them. Then, in a quiet voice, she responded, "It was me, Pastor Graetz."

He went on to preach about the boycott that Sunday, and the Graetzes would become one of the few white families in Montgomery that publicly supported it. This was a dangerous thing to do, as many white people viewed the white people who supported civil rights as "race traitors" and attacked them for their beliefs.

When Jo Ann Robinson arrived back on campus to teach her Friday class, she had a message to report to the president's office. Alabama State College president H. Councill Trenholm had learned of the leaflets—and he was furious. Robinson was exhausted from the all-nighter she'd pulled, and she was worried she'd be fired. But she summoned her resolve: "I described the frequent repetition of these outrages, how many children, men, and women, old and middle-aged people, had been humiliated and made to relinquish their seats to white people." Trenholm softened. Robinson promised not to use the college's space or resources for any more boycott activities and said she'd pay back the institution for the cost of producing the leaflets.

■   ■   ■

Nearly fifty ministers and other local leaders, including physicians, teachers, and union leaders, were at the meeting that evening. Rosa Parks was nervous as she approached the church, wondering if the community would support her. "I didn't know whether my getting arrested was going to set well or ill with the . . . leaders of the Black community." At first, the answer seemed to be no. The meeting began poorly. Nixon had put a minister named Roy Bennett in charge, and he lectured at the people gathered for thirty minutes without even mentioning

Parks or the boycott. People started to leave. Even Dr. King joked with a friend that he wanted to leave, but he couldn't because they were sitting in his church.

Finally, other people had the chance to speak. Parks addressed the group, explaining that she had reached her breaking point with segregation. Jo Ann Robinson also took the floor and spoke about the need to take action. Ultimately, the ministers, who did not want to abandon a Christian woman in need, agreed to promote the one-day boycott.

The "good Christian woman" image of Parks would grow in the weeks and months ahead. People highlighted her physical appearance: "above all . . . a lady," one boycotter described her. King referred to her as an "attractive seamstress," noting her radiant personality and how she was "soft-spoken and calm in all situations." He went on to describe her character as "impeccable" and her dedication as "deep-rooted." The Black newspaper the *Chicago Defender* referred to Parks as "the attractive little spark" that ignited the boycott. Radio interviews fixated on how she dressed. One radio interviewer gushed that Parks was "one of the most serene, one of the most beautiful women we've had the honor to meet," detailing her "beautiful straw hat" and "very smart dressmaker suit." Parks fit a particular kind of respectable feminized image, and people liked to highlight it.

That weekend before the boycott, many longtime Montgomery activists worried about whether Black people would actually band together and boycott the buses on Monday. One of Rosa Parks's old friends from the NAACP, J. E. Pierce, didn't support the boycott at first because he thought people wouldn't actually stay off the buses—and he felt it would be humiliating to the Black community when they didn't. Even Dr. King, who was new in town, was struck by the "appalling lack of unity" he saw in Montgomery's Black community and feared the division "could only be cured by some miracle." Of course, this division was rooted in fear: Black people knew that white people would do nearly anything to maintain the racial status quo, and they feared risking their lives or their livelihoods to press for change.

That Saturday, Parks was discouraged when only five Youth Council members showed up for her workshop. She later found out the reason they'd been absent was because they were handing out leaflets for the boycott on Monday. Mrs. Parks had taught them well.

But she didn't know any of this at the time, and anxiety was creeping up on her. She had no idea what Monday would bring.

# CHAPTER THIRTEEN

# ROSA PARKS GOES TO COURT

The Parkses, the Nixons, and the Kings woke up early Monday morning to see if people had stayed off the buses. And they had!

Nearly every Black person in Montgomery had stayed off the bus. It was a tremendous sight: the streets and sidewalks of Montgomery filled with Black men, women, and children walking, waiting, offering rides to people they knew or had never met.

Parks was elated, but she couldn't help wondering why it had taken so long for people to stand together in action.

Rosa had her court hearing that morning. They had timed the boycott around it.

She dressed carefully for the hearing, wearing "a straight, long-sleeved black dress with a white collar and cuffs, a small black velvet hat with pearls across the top and a charcoal-gray coat." For Mrs. Parks, this dignified image was a loud challenge to the

Going into court with Raymond for her trial

degrading nature of segregation. She would show that she wouldn't be intimidated.

She, Raymond, and Nixon met at Fred Gray's law office at 8:00 a.m. to figure out the last-minute details and then walked the block and half over to the courthouse. "I was not especially nervous," Parks said. "I knew what I had to do."

When they arrived at the courthouse, they were surprised to see a crowd. Black Montgomerians weren't exactly known for flocking to the building—nothing good had ever happened there for Black people.

But that morning, people lined the streets, the court-house steps, and the corridors of the building. Some of Parks's Youth Council members were in the crowd. One young woman called out, "They've messed with the wrong one now!" The crowd turned her words into a small chant and cheered when Rosa Parks, accompanied by Raymond, entered the building.

Pleased and astounded, Nixon later said, "It was the first time I had seen so much courage among our people!" Still, he was worried that the police would find any excuse to attack, and he cautioned the crowd that they shouldn't "even throw a cigarette butt" or "spit on the sidewalk or nothing."

In the courtroom, which was itself segregated, Parks, Gray, and the city prosecutor stood. And the trial didn't even last half an hour. Although Parks had been booked on a city charge, the prosecutor asked to have it changed to a state charge. (He was worried the original charges could be thrown out; a city law, passed in 1900 after an earlier Black bus boycott but rarely enforced, said that Black passengers couldn't be asked to move if there were no open seats in the back.)

This was a devious maneuver, and Gray objected. But the judge sided with the prosecutor, and the charges were changed.

Rosa Parks was found guilty.

Rosa Parks, E. D. Nixon, and Fred Gray after court

"It was a very emotional experience," Gray said, "because not only was I representing Mrs. Parks as her attorney, but we were friends. In addition, this was my first case with a large audience. . . . Was I nervous? Maybe a little. Was I determined? You bet."

After the hearing, Parks didn't go home but instead

went back to Gray's law office to help him. Typical of her personality, she wanted to be useful. He asked her to answer phones, because he had a meeting. So she spent the afternoon fielding calls about the boycott. But she decided to remain anonymous. "The people were calling to talk to me, but I never told them who I was," she admitted decades later. "They didn't know my voice, so I just took the messages."

The meeting Fred Gray attended that afternoon was the beginning of the Montgomery Improvement Association (MIA), a group that was formed to coordinate the boycott. Despite their key roles in the boycott, neither Parks nor Jo Ann Robinson was invited to participate. In fact, Parks was back answering Gray's phones while these decisions were being made. And despite the multiple roles women would play as organizers, fundraisers, and boycotters, the formal leadership of the boycott would be overwhelmingly male.

That afternoon, many of the ministers were nervous about speaking at the mass meeting planned for that evening and being publicly associated with the boycott. Finally, Nixon exploded in anger: "Where are the men? We need to turn history around and stop hiding behind these women who do all the work for us." Nixon understood that it was women who would be the foot soldiers of the boycott. They were the ones staying off the buses that day because most worked in white homes across town—and they were also the backbone of many of these congregations.

Nixon then threatened to take the microphone and tell their congregations that these clergy were "too cowardly to stand on their feet and be counted." King, who entered late, said he wasn't a coward and agreed to step forward publicly.

That afternoon, the participants chose Dr. King to lead the new group, partly because he was fairly new in town and hadn't made enemies in the various segments of Montgomery's Black community, as E. D. Nixon had. The only woman elected was Erma Dungee, as financial secretary.

That night, a huge crowd packed into Holt Street Baptist Church. It was so crowded that thousands of people couldn't even fit and had to stand outside. The church turned on its outdoor loudspeakers so the people gathered there could listen. Rosa Parks herself had trouble getting inside.

Once she did, she sat on the pulpit at the front of the church. Upon seeing the crowd, several ministers decided

Front page of the *Montgomery Advertiser*, December 6, 1955

Rosa Parks and
Martin Luther King Jr.

to make speeches, as did E. D. Nixon. Dr. King was quite
nervous. He hadn't had time to prepare a speech, but
once he started speaking, he became comfortable. He
spoke of a time "when people get tired. We are here to
say to those who have mistreated us so long that we are
tired—tired of being segregated and humiliated, tired of
being kicked about by the brutal feed of oppression." He
concluded with prophetic words about the historical sig-
nificance of what they were doing: "Right here in Montgomery, when the history books are written in the future,
somebody will have to say, 'There lived a great people—a
Black people—who injected new meaning and dignity
into the veins of civilization.'"

People were so stunned by the power of his speech,
they were silent for a moment after he finished. Then they
rose to their feet, cheering and clapping. After he finished

speaking, King hugged Rosa Parks. Outside, the crowd erupted into thunderous applause.

Following Dr. King's speech, Reverend Edgar N. French presented Parks as "the victim of this gross injustice" to the crowd. He stressed her reputation as a lady, "and any gentleman would allow a lady to have a seat." The crowd rose to its feet and gave her a standing ovation that lasted several minutes. People cheered in the audience: "Speak! Speak! Speak!"

But Mrs. Parks didn't speak that night. Given all the cheering, she asked those sitting up front with her if she should speak. Someone said she didn't need to, that she'd "said enough." Many years later, she told Highlander leader Myles Horton, "I think everyone spoke but me," though "it didn't bother me at that point." Reverend Graetz saw the decision not to have Parks speak as a gender issue: "Her personality was diminished. It was a male-dominated movement."

If Parks had spoken, she might have connected her resistance to the injustices perpetrated on the Scottsboro Boys, Recy Taylor, Jeremiah Reeves, and Emmett Till. She might have linked her protest to the courageous work being done at Highlander Folk School or by her own Youth Council members. She might have thanked the massive crowd for turning her individual refusal into a collective protest. She might have even said this movement was a long time coming, but what a joyful and holy day it was, now that it had arrived. She might have said all of this and more because this is what she knew. But she didn't get to speak.

The community felt so empowered by the success of the day's boycott that they decided to keep it going. The

Montgomery Improvement Association's demands were modest, at first: they wanted respectful treatment on the bus, along with first-come, first-served seating, and they wanted Black bus drivers to be hired. These demands changed over the course of the boycott, but initially, they did not include full desegregation of the bus.

Two years before the Montgomery bus boycott, Black residents of Baton Rouge, Louisiana, had launched a weeklong bus boycott and won some changes to bus segregation in their city, including opening more seats for Black people. Nixon and Parks had monitored it obsessively, excited by the Baton Rouge protest. The Montgomery organizers imagined they might be able to win some changes quickly if they kept their demands moderate like Baton Rouge had.

The demand to hire Black bus drivers likely stemmed from a visit the previous month by New York congressman Adam Clayton Powell Jr. E. D. Nixon had invited the Black politician to address the Progressive Democratic Association he was now running. Powell had helped organize "Don't Buy Where You Can't Work" campaigns in the 1930s, which targeted businesses that didn't hire Black employees. And in 1941, he'd helped organize a successful bus boycott that led to the hiring of two hundred Black drivers in New York City. He reminded his Montgomery audience of the power of "Black economic pressure."

They took his words to heart . . .

. . . and less than a month later, they tried it in their own city.

# CHAPTER FOURTEEN

# A YEARLONG BOYCOTT

One of the city's first responses to the boycott was to portray the problem as the actions of a handful of "bad apple" bus drivers. Officials insisted the problem was not segregation but rude drivers. City leaders said they wished the Black community had approached them sooner with the problem so they could have disciplined these drivers. Of course, this wasn't true at all. Black people had been highlighting bus segregation that entire year and even before then, and each time, they'd been ignored. But this way, the city was able to blame the issue on a few bad people rather than a rotten system.

Next, city officials acted as if bus segregation was not a matter of rights but a simple difference of opinion. In their discussions with Dr. King and the other boycott leaders, the city decided to include a member of the racist White Citizens' Council (WCC). When King protested, he was treated by city officials as if he was being "unreasonable." City leaders treated him and the Montgomery

Improvement Association and the racist White Citizens' Council (WCC) as if they were simply two different interest groups whose opposing views needed to be balanced.

The WCC had been founded in the months following the Supreme Court's *Brown v. Board of Education* decision by middle-class and upper-class white people, mostly in the South, who abhorred the possibility of desegregation. The group saw the Ku Klux Klan (KKK) as too low class, and they presented their members as more respectable. The WCC members preferred to use their wealth and political pressure rather than violence to silence attempts at desegregation—meaning they went after people's jobs and businesses, white or Black, if they seemed in favor of desegregation in any way. The WCC often included city leaders, police officers, and judges. And though the group prided itself on being more respectable than the KKK, some members of the WCC secretly engaged in violence too.

If one of the myths about Rosa Parks is that she was an accidental heroine, the other myth spun by Montgomery's white community at the time was that she was a plant arranged by people from outside the city and that her case was inauthentic. Multiple rumors rippled through the white community in the early weeks of the boycott: *She'd been planted by the NAACP or the Communist Party or both. Parks was Mexican. She didn't even live in Montgomery. She owned a car.* At base, these rumors framed her as an outsider and as someone un-American. According to Martin Luther King Jr., the argument among white Montgomery residents that the NAACP was behind Parks's actions was "so persistent and persuasive" that "it convinced many reporters from all across the country."

The bus boycott took place in the middle of the Cold War between the United States and the Soviet Union (USSR), which meant these accusations against Parks were dangerous. The US and USSR had come out of World War II as rivals; this came to be known as the Cold War because it was often fought through political means or through intervening in other countries, rather than direct military conflict between the US and USSR. Many Americans believed the USSR was trying to weaken the US from within, so people were fired for being affiliated with the Communist Party. People who criticized American policies and pointed out American racism were also seen as divisive and dangerous. So painting Rosa Parks as un-American was a way to cast doubt on the motives of the boycott and portray its leaders as possible traitors.

This didn't make sense, though. One way the United States portrayed its opposition to the USSR was that it upheld values of justice, democracy, and the rights to free speech and religion and the USSR did not. Yet people who criticized American race relations and the limits of these freedoms within the United States, particularly for people of color, were often portrayed as possible Soviet allies.

To combat these false accusations, Black leaders and the Black media started to bury Rosa Parks's long political history (even though it had been key to why people trusted her in the first place). They worried that her history with the NAACP could become a liability for the movement. The NAACP was being targeted by many Southern states as a potentially un-American organization. So leaders began to describe her as "a good Christian seamstress." Even Rosa Parks would go along with this image to keep the movement safe. So, though these myths of Parks as a one-day resister rather than a longtime political activist live on today, they began, in part, during the boycott to protect Parks and the movement.

One popular image of the Montgomery bus boycott is of people walking—and they certainly did. But Black Montgomerians were able to sustain a community-wide bus boycott for more than a year because they developed a massively well-organized car-pool system. The MIA had set up forty pickup stations throughout the city. People would meet at these spots to get a ride across town to work, to the doctor, to go shopping, or to attend church. People used the "V" for victory sign to identify themselves to riders and drivers supporting the boycott. The whole movement was run and organized by Black people.

Organizers passed around slips of paper at meetings asking:

*Can you drive in a car pool?*

*Do you own your car? Insurance?*

*What hours will you serve?*

*Who will drive your car?*

Three hundred people volunteered their cars. Johnnie Carr drove for the car pool, explaining, "Those of us who had automobiles felt that if other people who did not have cars would sacrifice and walk, we could certainly sacrifice our time and use our automobiles to help transport these people." Jo Ann Robinson also volunteered, driving for the car pool alongside teaching at Alabama State. Ultimately, the MIA provided fifteen thousand to twenty thousand rides per day.

Police stalked the car-pool pickup locations.

The police harassed the car pools mercilessly. Officers sat at the pickup stations and pulled over each car that came through in an effort to intimidate drivers, handing out hundreds of tickets for real and imagined violations. The MIA had to keep changing the pickup locations because of this ongoing police harassment. Robinson got seventeen tickets within a few *months*—and when the tickets didn't scare her off, a police officer in a squad car threw a rock through the front window of her home. Another two men in police uniforms poured acid all over her car. Many other drivers would come outside to find vandalized vehicles: gas tanks were filled with sugar, and brakes were tampered with.

But part of what was so encouraging for longtime activists like Parks and Nixon was how poor, working-class, and middle-class Black people banded together to make the car pool work. Before the boycott, middle-class Black people had often avoided joining forces with poor people. But during the boycott, a lot of middle-class Black people drove for the car pool, transporting working-class and poor people. Or if they didn't drive, they allowed others to use their cars. Cars were a big status symbol for the people who could afford them, so this was an important sign of unity. Not only that, but people continued to volunteer their cars even as police harassment increased.

Over time, the Montgomery Improvement Association hired fifteen dispatchers and twenty full-time drivers, all of which was coordinated from a building on the edge of Montgomery called the Citizens Club. With money from various churches, the MIA also bought fifteen station wagons, which became known as "rolling churches." They were painted with the names of churches, which helped sponsor them. The MIA also held mass meetings every week, which served as a way for people to share information, make plans, and maintain morale. The meetings became powerful community fundraisers too.

Though many of its visible leaders were men, the boycott was powered by women. They stayed off the buses, they attended the mass meetings, and they did much of the fundraising. Most of these women worked in white people's homes, and for many, they had to keep

Car pool!

their work for the boycott quiet or else they risked losing their jobs.

Early on in the boycott, a cook named Georgia Gilmore decided with her friends to try to raise money for all the costs the MIA was incurring through the car pool. None of them had a lot of money, but they began to sell sandwiches, dinners, pies, and cakes to raise money each week. They became known as the Club from Nowhere and presented the money they raised each week in the mass meetings. Because of these efforts, Gilmore was fired from her job at the National Lunch Company. But she was committed to her activism, so she began to cook from her home, which became a meeting and eating place. Dr. King even supported the Club from Nowhere's efforts, sometimes eating at her home diner.

The Club from Nowhere worked as an underground network of cooks because some couldn't afford to be publicly identified for fear of losing their jobs, as Gilmore had. "So when we made our financial reports to the MIA officers," Gilmore explained, "we had them record us as the money coming from nowhere. 'The Club from Nowhere.'"

Another group of women, headed by Inez Ricks, called themselves the Friendly Club and began their own bake sales to support the boycott. Something of a competition developed between the two groups, and each Monday both clubs would present their fundraising income at the mass meeting to a standing ovation.

■ ■ ■

Rosa Parks herself briefly served as a dispatcher for the carpool. Her instructions to riders encouraged patience:

Rosa Parks's notes about the car pool

"Remember how long some of us had to wait when the buses passed us without stopping in the morning and evening." She advised the drivers that "the riders may create some problems, but . . . they are making the protest the success that it is," and she told them to pick up as many people as possible and to "be careful," given the way police officers were harassing the carpools.

The visible leaders of the boycott—like King, Nixon, Graetz, and Parks—were receiving regular hate calls and death threats. The Kings' home was bombarded with calls *day and night*. Sometimes, when people called in the middle of the night to threaten "that n—r who's running the bus boycott," Coretta Scott King told them, "My husband is asleep. . . . He told me to write the name and number of anyone who called to threaten his life so that he could return the call and receive the threat in the morning when he wakes up and is fresh." So were the Parkses. Rosa's mother took to talking on the phone for hours just to keep the line busy.

Most of the MIA's leaders were young: King was twenty-six years old when the boycott began; Abernathy was twenty-nine and Gray was twenty-five. While women played crucial organizing and fundraising roles, they continued to be largely excluded from the formal leadership of the organization. According to Reverend Graetz, Parks attended the weekly mass meetings but was "treated like she didn't have anything to say."

Coretta Scott King also played a decisive role, though her leadership was rarely acknowledged. Eight weeks into the boycott, the Kings' home was bombed. Coretta and their ten-week-old baby, Yolanda, were home when the explosion went off, but they managed to escape unharmed. Dr. King rushed home as soon as he heard about the bomb.

Montgomery's police commissioner, Clyde Sellers, and the mayor, William Gayle, were some of the first people to arrive on the scene. Some thought they showed up right away because they knew the bombing was coming and hoped Black people would react by striking back, which would have given the city an excuse to crush the boycott.

Hundreds of Black people began to gather outside the Kings' home. Frightened and angry but able to channel courage and conviction, Dr. King came outside and quieted the crowd. "Brothers and sisters," he said, "we believe in law and order. Don't get panicky. . . . Don't get your weapons. . . . I want it to be known the length and breadth of this land that if I am stopped, this movement will not stop."

According to observers, Commissioner Sellers and Mayor Gayle seemed disappointed by his reaction.

Terrified by the violence, both Martin's father and Coretta's father traveled to Montgomery to persuade the family—or at least Coretta and the baby—to leave. Coretta told them she wasn't going anywhere. Martin realized the courage it took to tell their families no. "You were the only one who stood with me," he told Coretta. The progression of the boycott might have been different if she had caved and agreed to leave.

The day after the bombing at the Kings' house, E. D. Nixon's house was also bombed. Nixon was away on a Pullman trip, and, thankfully, no one was hurt that time either. Rosa and Raymond rushed over to help clean up the mess and help Nixon's family get the house in order. According to a friend, the couple was "part of a cleanup crew of people that would essentially help people whose homes had been bombed."

Black activists became more fearful after this violence. Parks asked the MIA to post night watchmen at her apartment, saying "strange men have been coming into my neighborhood inquiring about this woman who caused all this trouble." The MIA agreed to do so. Parks wrote a friend they were "more determined than ever" but "praying for courage and determination to withstand all attempts of intimidation."

Her neighbors at Cleveland Court likely also played a significant role in saving Parks's apartment from being attacked; people were around at all times of the day and night, which was a buffer that King, Abernathy, Nixon, and Graetz did not have, as they lived in houses.

According to Jo Ann Robinson, police officers (or men *dressed* as police officers) were responsible for a great deal of the violence against the boycott. And they got creative, employing these dirty tactics:

- Throwing paint and manure on houses
- Tossing bricks through windows
- Destroying yards and vehicles
- Scattering nails on streets to puncture tires

Crosses were even burned on the campus of Alabama State College, where Jo Ann Robinson worked.

The FBI took note of the violence in Montgomery but chose not to investigate. Its agents expressed no problem with the Montgomery Police Department's inability or unwillingness to identify any suspects. The FBI simply sent a message to national headquarters that said:

## BOYCOTT CONTINUING

During the civil rights movement, the FBI actively hurt the struggle in two ways: One, they took little interest in white violence against Black activists; sometimes they knew about the violent acts before they happened, and still they did nothing. Two, the FBI was also suspicious of Black activists like Martin Luther King and groups like the MIA, and so they began to monitor their activities.

The FBI began monitoring Dr. King during the boycott.

■ ■ ■

Because of the boycott, the bus company was suffering financially. A month after Rosa Parks's arrest, the company was forced to raise fares, lay off dozens of drivers, and cut off many bus routes. White people in Montgomery began organizing their own anti-boycott, calling on other whites to ride the buses to support the company's stand on segregation.

The *Montgomery Advertiser* newspaper was extremely critical of the boycott in its reporting. And the White Citizens' Council (WCC) increased the pressure against the boycott. They circulated flyers urging people to ride the bus, and in February, two months after the boycott had begun, they held a massive rally. Waving Confederate flags, WCC members spoke of "states' rights" and giving "the n—s a whipping" with a particularly "harsh lesson" for Rosa Parks. They canvassed neighborhoods, targeting any whites who seemed to be wavering.

The city, too, used several tactics to try to break up the boycott. When all the traffic tickets didn't stop it, the city dredged up an old anti-boycott law as a way to try to target the leadership. On February 21, 1956, it indicted 115 boycott leaders, including King, Nixon, Robinson, and Parks. (The number of indictments later dropped to eighty-nine.) The FBI also took note of the indictments and sent the full list to Washington, DC.

King, who'd turned twenty-seven years old on January 15, was now a cherished leader in the Black community, particularly among many older women who did domestic work in white homes and were the backbone of the boycott. They were exceedingly proud that such a brave, young leader had emerged in their midst, and they defended him to the hilt, even when it meant challenging their white employers who insisted King was only out for himself.

"Efforts were being made to have [Martin Luther King] bear the blame for the boycott," Reverend Solomon Seay said. Not wanting King to shoulder all the blame, many of the indicted group decided to turn themselves in to the police rather than wait to be arrested. Parks, along with Nixon, was one of the first to show up. "Are you looking for me?" she said to the sheriff. "Well, I am here." This was the largest indictment in Alabama history. As person after person was booked, the atmosphere outside the county courthouse, where a large group of Black people had gathered to witness these activists going in, was proud and determined.

E. D. Nixon mug shot, 1956

Jo Ann Robinson mug shot, 1956

Rosa Parks mug shot, 1956

Martin Luther King Jr. mug shot, 1956

Fred Gray mug shot, 1956

The mood that day was quite different from how it was the night of Rosa Parks's first arrest two and a half months earlier. "We were surrounded by crowds of people," she recalled. "And reporters and photographers all across the country were on hand, and when I went in to be fingerprinted and arrested, there was a photographer to take our pictures and we had such a spirit of unity that there were people who felt somewhat left out when they were not among those arrested."

One interviewer asked if it was "more popular to be arrested the second time than the first?"

"Yes," Parks replied. "The first time I was very much alone because none on the bus who witnessed my arrest volunteered to accompany me or show sympathy in any way."

The mug shot of Parks taken that February day, bearing number 7053—along with a photo of her being fingerprinted by police officer Drue Lackey—would become iconic.

While Parks and the others were inside, the crowd, many of whom carried shotguns, started to get restless. In turn, the police grew tense. Reverend B. J. Simms described the scene:

Black women with bandannas on, wearing men's hats with their dresses rolled up. From the alleys they came. This is what frightened white people. Not the collar and tie group. One of the police hollered, "All right, you women get back." These great big old women with their dresses rolled up told him, and I never will forget their language, "Us ain't going nowhere. You done arrested us preachers and we ain't moving. . . . If you hit one of us, you'll not leave here alive."

The city's tactic had backfired.

City leaders had hoped the indictments would scare the Black community into submission. Instead, it strengthened their resolve. The MIA's demands expanded to *full desegregation on the bus system.*

The boycott had widened the possibility of what people thought they could achieve. They wouldn't just settle for better treatment—they wanted full equality. As Parks herself had learned over the years, taking action expanded the kind of just society she could imagine and demand. Now the community was finding this out themselves.

The indictment of eighty-nine boycott leaders was so extreme that the national media, like the *New York Times* and the *Washington Post*, started to take note of what was happening in Montgomery. The picture of Parks being fingerprinted made international news.

And for the first time since the boycott had begun, they sent journalists down to Montgomery to report on what was happening.

# CHAPTER FIFTEEN

# THE BEST OF TIMES AND THE WORST OF TIMES

The boycott was gaining visibility, but at work, Rosa Parks's coworkers "ignore[d] me like I wasn't there." Many of the women in the alterations department who worked in the room next to her "refused to have any conversation or to speak to me at all."

Five weeks after her arrest, Parks was fired from her job at Montgomery Fair.

The department store claimed it was closing the tailor shop because the tailor was leaving, so the store would have no need for her services. Never mind that Parks was skilled enough to have taken over his job or that she could have been given another job at the store. Instead, Montgomery Fair dismissed her.

A week later, Raymond's employer, the Maxwell Air Force Base barbershop, forbade any talk about the boycott or "that woman." Part of being a barber meant talking with customers, so not being able to discuss his wife was insulting to a proud, political man like Raymond Parks.

So Raymond was forced to resign from his job.

Shortly after they both lost their jobs, their rent at Cleveland Court was raised by ten dollars. The Parks family was in serious financial trouble, and neither Rosa nor Raymond would find steady work in Montgomery ever again. A month later, recognizing their desperate financial situation, Dr. King ordered a one-time payment of three hundred dollars from the MIA to the Parks family.

The Parkses' phone rang constantly with death threats and terrible insults. "There were people who called to say that I should be beaten or killed," Parks recalled, "because I was causing so much trouble." After she was fired, one woman called just to laugh at her.

Raymond was angry and deeply frustrated. They ran out of money and were forced to close their bank account. He took out a loan on his life insurance, which he and Rosa paid back, little by little. The death threats didn't let up, and it was hard on Raymond to be home answering hateful calls instead of out working. Rosa said he was shaken and very upset "because we had lived under this tension for so long."

Raymond started sleeping with his gun.

He was "furious" at many things during the year of the boycott, according to Rosa: furious at himself "for being a financial failure," at the bus driver "for causing [her] arrest," and at Rosa herself for being stubborn and a "goat head" and not just getting off the bus instead of making her stand. Raymond told her *he* would have gotten off the bus at the driver's order to move, favoring his dignity and safety over direct action. Raymond took to drinking and smoking a lot to soothe his troubles.

There is sometimes a tendency today to look back on the civil rights movement and paint the activists as endlessly able to take whatever was thrown at them. But that wasn't true. Rosa Parks never sugarcoated the fact that living through that time was like being in a war zone, and Raymond's reaction to the exceedingly difficult times was normal. The year of the boycott was harder on Raymond, she felt, because he was home answering the hate calls and worrying about their poverty. They lived with constant stress and fear.

While physical violence was one method of preserving segregation, another way white people tried to do this was by getting people fired and by making it impossible for civil rights activists to find steady work again. But this tactic, and the suffering the Parks family endured, isn't often included in the public stories of Rosa Parks taught today.

Meanwhile, Rosa Parks was traveling more and more, raising attention and funds for the boycott. Because of the car pool, the Montgomery Improvement Association needed money to buy more cars, pay for gas, and coordinate the dispatching. The MIA sent Parks all over the country to raise money for the boycott: Detroit, Seattle, California, New York, and Indiana. She brought the story of what was happening in Montgomery to Black people and white allies across the country, turning a local struggle into a national one. Clifford Durr described her as one of their best fundraisers. Spreading the word about the boycott far and wide took a lot of hard work, and she worried about her family and their growing poverty.

Part of how she kept going was her faith and reliance on prayer: "I prayed hard not to give in and not to fall hard by the wayside." Parks had long been a devoted member of St. Paul AME Church. In January, while praying at church, she experienced a profound sense of religious conviction and a sense that all that was happening—her stand, the boycott—was God's plan. All she needed to do was "keep the faith." A sense of intense calm washed over her.

**FIRST TIME IN BALTIMORE!**

HEAR!— **MRS. ROSA PARKS**

Whose arrest, because she refused to be segregated, led to the Bus Boycott in Montgomery, Alabama.

**BALTIMORE BRANCH N.A.A.C.P.**
**KICK-OFF**
**MASS MEETING**

**SUNDAY, SEPTEMBER 23, 1956 - 3 P.M.**
**SHARP STREET METHODIST CHURCH**
Dolphin and Etting Streets
——Music by Famous BALTIMORE CHORALE——
under direction of Gerald Burkes Wilson

**RENEW YOUR MEMBERSHIP TODAY!**
And Get One More!

*Good Music*                    *Admission Free*
Mrs. Lillie M. Jackson, President          Dr. Charles Watts, Treasurer

Rosa Parks traveled the country raising attention and funds for the boycott. This is a flyer from her Baltimore appearance in 1956.

Her own mental determination also sustained her: "I have learned over the years that when one's mind is made up, this diminishes fear." Crisscrossing the country from Baltimore to Los Angeles, she urged perseverance in her speeches, saying, "One day we will have the democracy we are hoping for." She promised to "continue in every way I can."

Part of what sustained Rosa was also support from Horton and Clark at Highlander and many of the people she had met at the workshop. Horton and Clark had been delighted by the "militant unity" on display in Montgomery—and invited Parks back to Highlander

Rosa's mom came with her on one of her trips to Highlander. Here they are with Septima Clark.

numerous times that year to share the story of the ongoing boycott with other organizers and strategize with Highlander supporters and other activists about keeping the movement going. Mrs. Parks would become one of Highlander's best supporters, even as the school came under harassment from the government, which portrayed them as having ties to Communists.

Rosa found the travel exhilarating but also exhausting. In her speeches, she spoke of how she was reading about earlier freedom fighters, like Crispus Attucks, Harriet Tubman, Phillis Wheatley, and Mary McLeod Bethune, and how they all had the courage to stand by their convictions. Parks knew she stood on the shoulders of ancestors, and that gave her the strength to keep going; reading about Black history had always energized her to keep pushing forward.

In March 1956, Rosa Parks boarded her first airplane. She'd been invited to Detroit to speak to Local 600, a radical branch of the United Auto Workers. The national head of the autoworkers union, Walter Reuther, was opposed to Local 600 bringing her, but the Detroit members wouldn't take no for an answer, raising money on their own to pay for her visit. They put her up in the Garfield Hotel in Paradise Valley, a Black section of Detroit. Like in Alabama, most hotels in the city did not serve Black people.

Two months later, in May, Parks set off on her first visit to New York City. The two-week trip was thrilling! Parks toured Harlem with Ella Baker and went to meetings with Dr. Kenneth Clark, whose research had been pivotal to the Supreme Court's decision in *Brown v. Board of Education*. She got to meet a number of her heroes, including A. Philip Randolph, leader of the Brotherhood of Sleeping Car Porters, and NAACP executive secretary Roy Wilkins. She also spent an evening with Thurgood Marshall, the NAACP lawyer who'd been one of the legal forces behind the *Brown* decision, along with his wife, Cecilia. Mrs. Parks and the King family stayed out with the Marshalls until one-thirty in the morning. She also did some sightseeing, including a visit to the Statue of Liberty. "We went to the top of it, twenty-two stories," she wrote home to her mother. Rosa Parks's life had changed in ways she never could have imagined six months earlier.

On May 24, she spoke at a massive civil rights rally and fundraiser at Madison Square Garden in New York City. Ella Baker and others had worked for six weeks to pull off the "Heroes of the South" event. The Garden was packed with *sixteen thousand* people—much to the surprise of the Black newspaper the *Pittsburgh Courier*, which noted that the space was rarely used for political events, given how big it was and difficult to fill.

Dr. King was supposed to headline the event but had to cancel. So Parks and Nixon represented the boycott instead. The other guest speakers included former First Lady Eleanor Roosevelt, labor leader Randolph, Dr. T. R. M. Howard of the Till case, NAACP leader Wilkins, and Congressman Powell. The singer Sammy

Davis Jr., jazz singer and band leader Cab Calloway, and actress-singer Pearl Bailey also participated in the festivities. Parks told the crowd that if she had to do it all over again, she would still refuse to give up her seat. The event raised six thousand dollars, a lot of money for that time.

With such a full schedule, Parks still worried she was "needed in Montgomery." While she was in New York, Highlander leader Myles Horton arranged for her to meet with Eleanor Roosevelt. The former First Lady knew the consequences of taking bold stands in 1950s America, and she asked Parks if she'd been accused of being a Communist. Parks said yes. Both women knew firsthand that this was a common way of smearing civil rights activists, as both had been accused of having Communist sympathies for their racial justice work.

Roosevelt wrote about Parks in her newspaper column. Describing Rosa as "a very quiet, gentle persona," Roosevelt also said it was "difficult to imagine how she could take such a positive and independent stand," underestimating the substance of Parks's inner strength and determination. Throughout her life, Parks's shyness would be mistaken for meekness, when, in fact, she was bold to the core. Her friend Roberta Wright explained, "She's quiet—the way steel is quiet. . . . She seems almost meek, but we already know the truth of that, don't we?" Black journalist Vernon Jarrett agreed: "The contradictory personality that is Rosa Parks, that subdued thunder in her Southern country-woman's voice—did not prepare her listener for the little verbal bombs that she exploded."

Applauding Parks's bravery, the First Lady challenged the idea that her resistance had come out of nowhere:

"These things do not happen all of a sudden. They grow out of feelings that have been developing over many years. Human beings reach a point . . . and from then on it may be passive resistance, but it will be resistance."

Parks returned to Montgomery absolutely glowing with excitement over her trip and the "wonderful reception" she'd received. However, her health was suffering during this time. The stress of public scrutiny, the financial troubles her family faced, and the constant threat of violence that hung over them like a dark cloud gave her insomnia and ulcers. Still, she powered on.

In early June, she flew to San Francisco for the forty-seventh annual NAACP national convention. She was met by a white reporter who said he wanted "to take me apart and see what made me tick." He aggressively questioned her, accusing her of seeking publicity and calling her a prostitute. Parks grew so upset she began shaking. Overwhelmed by the onslaught of hate, she broke down in "hysterics . . . I mean, I started screaming—I'll kill you—I just cried[.] That's the only time I had done that in a press conference." Pleased he had gotten under her skin, the reporter left. Parks sat there for another half hour crying.

In all her public appearances, this is the only time Rosa Parks or anyone else describes her losing her composure. Considering how much stress she'd faced for decades, and the many appearances she was making, her composure was *remarkable*. According to her niece Rhea, both her aunt Rosa and her own father, Sylvester, had learned "not to display their emotions, to always be in control of their faculties"—because of the dangers Black people faced if white people saw their full emotions. Parks probably internalized all this stress, likely contributing to her insomnia and ulcers.

In several ways, for Rosa Parks, the year of the boycott was both the best of times and the worst of times. She was able to experience so many new, incredible things, like her first plane rides, the chance to speak to huge groups of people about her important political work, and the opportunity to meet some of her heroes. She was thrilled by the unity and resolve of Montgomery's Black community and the ways people across the country were lending their support—especially after so many years of working toward this mass movement.

But she and Raymond were in deep financial trouble because of her bus stand, and she still feared for their safety. The Parkses' income tax records reveal how desperate their situation had grown: in 1955, they reported a total yearly income of $3,749, but by 1956, that number had fallen to $1,813. They didn't have a lot of money even before she was arrested; they couldn't afford a car and were living in public housing. But after the boycott began, their financial situation was a disaster. Nearly all the money Rosa raised as she traveled around the country went into funding the movement, whether that was the MIA or the NAACP. She and Raymond were having trouble making ends meet, but some male leaders of the boycott who were also speaking around the country had no trouble keeping a portion of the income for themselves.

Some friends and fellow activists were delighted for Rosa Parks, but others were jealous of the attention she was getting. Activists like Jo Ann Robinson and E. D. Nixon felt their contributions weren't being fully recognized, and they grew resentful. Many people—even her friends—didn't realize the financial crisis she and Raymond were facing. Rosa Parks was a deeply proud woman, and she didn't like to talk about her personal troubles.

Virginia Durr saw what was happening to Rosa, though. Virginia was no stranger to hard times, as she'd been shunned by most other white Alabamians for her support of civil rights. The bus boycott provided her with a larger purpose—and seeing the way the Parks family was struggling emboldened her. Durr wrote dozens of letters to friends and political associates across the country, letting them know about the boycott and asking for help for the Parks family. On her own, Durr raised around five hundred dollars.

Faced with mounting debt, a worsening ulcer, a sick mother, and a husband sinking further and further into despair, Parks reluctantly accepted the money. Durr wrote to a friend that Rosa was "so reserved and proud, if it were not by necessity, she wouldn't take a nickel in contribution."

Durr's money provided temporary stability for the Parks family. But by July, the money had run out, and, according to Durr, Parks was sewing on the side "for little or nothing . . . sort of like Cinderella." So Durr kept writing letters, managing to raise an additional $350 over the summer.

Unnerved by the constant harassment and their inability to find steady work, and drinking too much, Raymond suffered a nervous breakdown. Virginia Durr persuaded Rosa to take her husband to a psychiatrist at Maxwell Air Force Base. According to Durr, the psychiatrist felt Raymond "had no identity" and said that "if Mrs. Parks had been a more yielding, soft, and a kind of helpless woman, he might have found his identity in being a husband. . . . [The psychiatrist] thought Mrs. Parks ought to give up all her civil rights work and go back to being a little sweet housewife." Durr found the advice "absurd."

There is no record from Rosa Parks or Raymond of this doctor visit or her reaction to it. But she did not give up her civil rights work, and she was always quick to note Raymond's support of her, which may suggest he didn't accept this psychiatrist's thinking either. Rosa thought of Raymond's difficulties as similar to the type of trauma a soldier might suffer from battle. Worried that others saw his challenges as weird or weak, she emphasized how much most people were hurt from such unrelenting stress.

Raymond's pain manifested more visibly, but the stress also took its toll on Rosa and many others during the boycott. In addition to her painful stomach ulcers, she also developed a heart condition that would plague her for many years. She suffered from chronic insomnia, a problem she'd been dealing with since she was a young child when the Ku Klux Klan would ride through Pine Level. Her mother, Leona, was also not well for many months of the boycott year, and E. D. Nixon developed high blood pressure. But Rosa Parks didn't talk about the cost of fighting injustice. As a longtime friend of hers in Detroit later observed, she "never got into it much. You really have to pull things out of her."

Black Montgomerians weren't the only ones experiencing harassment and dealing with the toll it took. Across town, city librarian Juliette Morgan was one of the few white people, alongside the Durrs and Graetzes, who supported the boycott. Morgan's public solidarity with the protest, including writing a letter in defense of the boycott to the *Montgomery Advertiser*, led to unceasing harassment from other white people. They wanted her fired from her job, and some white people even wanted her dead. The library backed her at first, but they insisted that she not write anything else or participate in *any* civil rights work. When Morgan wrote another letter criticizing "cowardly Southern white men" for harassing the boycott and Autherine Lucy, a Black student who'd attempted to desegregate the University of Alabama, a flood of mental and physical harassment followed.

Juliette Morgan's harassment, according to Jo Ann Robinson, was "unending." For over a year, she dealt with hateful phone calls and with people lurking outside her home and throwing rocks at her windows. The White Citizens' Council even succeeded in getting the library to force her resignation. Morgan lived with her mother, who was angry with her for taking such a stand and felt Juliette was ruining her life. Morgan consequently had a "nervous breakdown," according to Parks. A year and a half after the boycott began, Juliette Morgan took her own life. No Black Montgomerians were allowed to attend her funeral.

People who challenged society's racial boundaries, like Parks and Morgan, were, in effect, calling the whole system of white supremacy into question. Today, many of the core principles of the boycott—that bus segregation was a way to maintain economic and social power for white people and that it was morally, as well as legally, wrong—have been largely accepted. Most people now look back and assume they, too, would have boycotted, or written letters to the paper in favor of the boycott, or risked their jobs in support. But that overlooks how hard it was to stand up for equality and survive and the deep sacrifices it entailed.

As Nikki Giovanni writes in her poem "Harvest":

... Something needs to be said ... about Rosa Parks ...
... other than her feet ... were tired
... Lots of people. ... on that bus ... and many before. ...
and since ... had tired feet. ...
Lots of people ... still do. ...
they just don't know where. ... to plant them.

# CHAPTER SIXTEEN

# VICTORY AT LAST (BUT THE STRUGGLE CONTINUES)

**M**ontgomery activists had learned from experience the lengths the State of Alabama would go to in order to ensure segregation wasn't challenged.

One way was to prevent legal appeals from ever being heard in state court. This was what happened with Viola White's case in the 1940s, and activists feared it would happen again with Rosa Parks. So her attorney, Fred Gray, decided to file a new case against Montgomery's bus segregation—this time in *federal* court.

Four women who'd encountered discrimination on Montgomery's buses—Aurelia Browder, Susie McDonald, Claudette Colvin, and Mary Louise Smith—agreed to be part of the lawsuit. The thirty-seven-year-old Browder, who was a midwife and rode the buses regularly, had been arrested a month after Colvin. As with Parks's arrest, Browder's was not her first act of bus resistance.

Susie McDonald was a senior citizen who had also resisted mistreatment on the bus. Gray had wanted a minister to be part of the case, but none of them were willing to step forward—even though two teenagers, Colvin and Smith, summoned the courage. "Our leaders are just we ourselves," Colvin would testify in the case. A fifth woman, Jeanetta Reese, was originally on the suit but pulled out a day after it was filed, after both she and her husband were threatened.

Gray filed the suit, *Browder v. Gayle*, on February 1, 1956. In the end, Parks was not part of the federal case. Gray was worried that if she were, the lawsuit could be tossed out on a technicality, because Parks already had a case pending in state court. Her long history with the NAACP may have also contributed to the decision. Because of the group's key role in school desegregation, the NAACP was increasingly targeted in the years after *Brown*. Public officials opposed to desegregation portrayed the organization as dangerous and potentially un-American in its challenge to US racism, implying the USSR might be behind them. (In fact, by June of 1956, the NAACP would be outlawed in Alabama as a "foreign" organization.) So, the possibility of having Rosa Parks's long history with the NAACP exposed could have been seen as a problematic part of their case. After all, the *Montgomery Advertiser* had written a long, negative article on E. D. Nixon's history with the group.

Surprisingly, on June 19, 1956, two out of three judges for the US Court for the Middle District of Alabama ruled in favor of the women's challenge that bus segregation was unconstitutional. Montgomery's Black community was ecstatic. The city and bus company were not happy, to say the least, and appealed the decision. So, the case headed to the US Supreme Court. On November 13, 1956, the high court unanimously upheld the lower court's ruling—which declared Montgomery's bus segregation illegal. Parks was speaking in Springfield, Massachusetts, that day when she got the news. Her speech notes read how "happy" she was to hear of the Supreme Court's decision but that there was "more work to be done" to actually implement desegregation and bolster the NAACP, which was under attack across the country.

The boycott, combined with Fred Gray's decision to start a case in federal court and the courage of the women plaintiffs, had worked!

On December 21, 1956, more than a year since the boycott had started, Montgomery's buses were desegregated. Black people could sit wherever they wanted.

Several media outlets traveled to Montgomery to capture the moment. Most focused on Dr. King, taking pictures of him getting on and off buses all day, and didn't even think of Parks. But *Look* magazine contacted her, wanting to photograph her on the bus. The publication staged a shot that would become the most famous

**Montgomery's Bus Boycott Comes to End**

Segregation Barriers Dropped as Court's Ruling Takes Effect

SUNNY AND MILD
**ALABAMA JOURNAL**
Latest Edition
EVENING TIME
IS READING TIME
*Central and Southeast Alabama's Largest Evening Newspaper*

48th YEAR—NO. 273    THE ASSOCIATED PRESS    MONTGOMERY, ALA., TUESDAY, NOVEMBER 13, 1956    UNITED PRESS    30 PAGES    PRICE FIVE CENTS

**BUS SEGREGATION IS KNOCKED OUT**

photo of Mrs. Parks—her "symbol shot," as she called it. In the photo, Rosa Parks sits in the front of the bus, looking out the window with a white man behind her. The man wasn't a Montgomery resident, though; he was reporter Nicholas Chriss. He later wrote: "A great scoop for me, but Mrs. Parks had little to say. She seemed to want to savor the event alone."

In the middle of the *Look* photo shoot, she and the people from the magazine boarded a bus driven by none other than James Blake, the man responsible for her arrest the previous year. The reporter was unaware of their connection, but Parks knew exactly who Blake was. And he seemed to know who she was too. They simply "ignored each other," Parks said.

E. D. Nixon later recalled the power of that day, saying he "cried like a baby." For Nixon, as for Parks, the successful end of the boycott was the result of more than a decade of painstaking struggle.

The end of the boycott did not mean the Black community was safe from white violence. Bus stops were attacked. So were the homes of the leaders—Dr. King's and Reverend Graetz's houses were bombed again. And the Parks family was still suffering; neither Rosa nor Raymond could find steady work, and they were still getting death threats.

One question facing the MIA was what injustice to attack next. Parks and Nixon wanted to start a statewide voter registration campaign in order to open up access and build Black political power in Alabama. They saw voter registration as the next key step after the boycott, given how most Black Alabamians were not registered to vote (though not for lack of trying by many) and thus denied the political power to protect themselves and their interests. Keeping Black people from voting helped further other injustices, like school segregation, job discrimination, and unpunished violence against Black people, since politicians didn't feel they had to be accountable to the interests of the Black community. Nixon and Parks wanted to run the project from Fred Gray's office, employing Parks full-time to coordinate it. Virginia Durr supported this idea and began writing her friends around the country to help out. But they had trouble gaining funding and support for the initiative.

Reverends King and Abernathy, however, wanted to go in a different direction. They considered a boycott of the airport, which Parks and Nixon thought was foolish, as few Black people even used it back then.

King and Abernathy were also looking to expand their work outside Montgomery. So, in January 1957, along with other politically active ministers like Reverend Fred Shuttlesworth of Birmingham and Reverend T. J. Jemison of Baton Rouge, they founded the Southern Christian Leadership Conference (SCLC). Their goal was to take the work they'd begun in Montgomery across the southern United States and "redeem the soul of the nation."

That spring, the divide between Nixon and King began to widen. Nixon had different ideas about what the MIA should tackle next; he also felt his own leadership role in the boycott was being overlooked amid all the attention King was getting. The differences between middle-class ministers and working-class people that had been set aside during the boycott reemerged in the aftermath. And Parks sided with Nixon.

Nixon realized Parks was in a desperate economic situation and pushed the MIA to hire her. The organization had the resources to do so, but it had hired other women instead. Virginia Durr wrote to a friend about the "blazing row" taking place within the MIA. Parks had "been a heroine everywhere else," Durr wrote, "[but] they have not given her a job here, although she needed one desperately. . . . She is very disgruntled with MLK and really quite bitter, which is not like her at all." To another friend, Durr explained, "They know she cannot get a job, they know she has suffered and is suffering, and they blandly do nothing about it at all, and this drives me nearly nuts and makes me distrust them very much indeed."

Along with Parks's need for a job, Nixon was also angry about the ways he was being treated by King and the other ministers, and he may have used Parks's situation to highlight the mistreatment of them both. A few months later, Nixon would leave the organization.

Friends had also tried to pressure Highlander to help Parks, but Clark and Horton felt that a separate fundraising effort for her would "backfire," and that it needed to come through the MIA.

The MIA had hired other women to work as administrative assistants, but these women had attended college and were also members of Dexter Avenue Baptist Church, where King was pastor. Though she knew how to type and was a seasoned organizer, a working-class woman like Rosa Parks, who attended a different church, was outside the social circles of men like King and Abernathy. Given the dated ideas of the time about gender roles, they may have also felt that Parks's difficult situation was her husband's responsibility and not theirs.

Rosa Parks didn't talk about this much in her later life. In fact, in most interviews, she covered up the tremendous difficulty of this period. But an early outline for her 1992 autobiography contained a description for a chapter that didn't appear in the final book. Entitled "In the Shadows," the summary reads:

> Jealousy and dissension within the Montgomery Improvement Association—Rosa Parks has lost her job at Montgomery Fair department store over the incident that sparked the boycott and feels that she should be given a job with the Montgomery Improvement Association—but King refuses and Rosa feels angry— she goes through extreme financial difficulties—by the time Rosa is offered a job in the voter registration drive that King decides to start, she has accepted a job at Hampton.

It is unclear if Parks or her cowriter, James Haskins, removed the chapter or if her publisher did so. Parks wasn't the type to air her issues publicly—partly because she was worried about it having a detrimental impact on the movement. So she may have decided she didn't want to publish this disagreement. Or her publisher may have thought the content was too negative and decided against running it.

■    ■    ■

Parks was still being invited to speak to NAACP chapters and other Black organizations around the country and traveling a lot. But by the summer of 1957, her spirits were quite low. She didn't want to ask for help or draw attention to her own problems, so she finally decided it was time to leave Montgomery. The decision also stemmed partly from negativity the Parks family encountered from other leaders, particularly some of the male ministers. A number had grown resentful of Parks's national stature and didn't understand why she was getting so much attention, and some made disparaging remarks about her and Raymond. Most didn't realize this national attention did little to alleviate the Parks family's desperate financial situation.

Rosa had grown bewildered by this animosity and frustrated with the divisions in the MIA. Her brother, Sylvester, had been urging her to join them in Detroit. And Raymond was now open to a change. Since Rosa's arrest and their tremendous financial difficulties, he was more willing to head somewhere new for a fresh start than he'd been in the past. Plus, the hate calls to their home persisted. So Rosa called her cousin Thomas Williamson in Detroit, and he wired three hundred dollars to help them make the trip north. It was the "best thing I could do at the time," Rosa said.

People in Montgomery were embarrassed when they learned the Parks family had decided to leave town. As E. D. Nixon observed many years later, "We had done the same thing the white man wanted. After the whites made it hard for her to get a job, all the doors closed on her and the Negroes kept them closed. . . . The point is that she should never have had to leave [Montgomery]."

Reverend Abernathy visited the Parkses' apartment to apologize and ask them to stay. The community raised five hundred dollars for the family and held a testimonial dinner in Mrs. Parks's honor at St. Paul AME Church as a farewell event. That night, she gave a powerful speech telling people to keep fighting "for the right of everyone to have opportunities, and not just themselves." She was very touched by the evening and the donations raised.

In August 1957, eight months after the boycott's end, the Parks family (Rosa, Raymond, and her mother, Leona) bid a bittersweet good-bye to Alabama and headed to Detroit. Almost as soon as they arrived, though, Rosa left for Hampton University in Virginia, where she'd been hired as a hostess at the school's inn.

Because many hotels did not serve Black people, Black colleges often ran their own to host university visitors. Rosa's willingness to move to Hampton without Raymond was a testament to how desperate they were for work. Hampton had promised it would, in time, provide her with family housing—but it never did. And while she loved being with the Hampton students, she didn't love her job there. She had constant work preparing for hotel guests, and she was lonely without her family. She was also quite sick, as her ulcers had flared up; she was having trouble eating solid food and lost a lot of weight. But the money she was making at Hampton was keeping her mother and Raymond afloat in Detroit. Leona wrote her encouraging letters, telling her daughter to stick it out.

The *Pittsburgh Courier* had discovered that Rosa Parks had been essentially forced to leave Montgomery. They had done a long interview with her right before she left Montgomery. In November, they ran a somewhat critical story on the situation. "She got no part of the money being paid out by the MIA—of which she was the direct cause!" reporter Trezzvant Anderson wrote. Describing her with "dimmed tears in her eyes" and "sick at heart," Anderson wrote that "not once did Rosa Parks grumble or complain."

Mrs. Parks didn't like this kind of attention. She wrote Raymond after the story was published, telling him she "felt sick" over it. She relayed how Jo Ann Robinson had sent her a "blistering carbon copy" of Robinson's response to the *Courier* about publishing such an article. A story that exposed her own suffering made Parks feel like she had compromised the movement.

She kept plugging away at Hampton, though she still found the work hard and isolating. She sent Raymond many letters about how much she missed him and how hard it was to be apart. Finally, she'd had enough, and after more than a year in Virginia, she moved back to Detroit, at the end of 1958, to be with her family.

# CHAPTER SEVENTEEN

# "THE NORTHERN PROMISED LAND THAT WASN'T"

R osa Parks is almost always associated with the South. If her move to Detroit is mentioned, it's usually painted as the happy ending to a difficult life in Montgomery.

But this was far from the case.

Parks would live more than half of her life in Detroit, what she called "the Northern promised land that wasn't." Just as she had in Montgomery, she took on the struggle against racism in her new hometown. In fact, she would spend the next *forty years* fighting racism in the North, though this is rarely acknowledged in stories about her life.

Often, narratives about the civil rights movement focus only on the South. Racism is portrayed as a regional illness rather than a national disease. The truth is, antiracist movements bloomed across the country, in cities as varied as Boston, Milwaukee, Los Angeles, New York, Seattle, and Detroit, because segregation and racial injustice were widespread across the country.

"The racial issue that we confront in America is not a sectional but a national problem," Dr. King said, speaking in New York City in 1960. Many white Northerners liked to present themselves as more racially progressive than Southerners; some pushed for change in the South, but most still preferred segregated neighborhoods and schools and reserved the best jobs for fellow white people in their own hometowns.

The Parks family was part of a stream of Black people who migrated from Alabama to Detroit during the middle of the twentieth century; Rosa's brother and cousins had moved there several years before she joined them. Detroit's Black population doubled in the 1940s and continued to grow throughout the 1950s and 1960s.

But, as Parks observed, the new city was no promised land. Thankfully, Detroit didn't have the public signs declaring segregation that Montgomery had, but Parks couldn't "find too much difference" in the white supremacist system that enforced segregated housing and schools, job discrimination, and abusive policing. Rosa and Raymond both struggled for years to find jobs or a decent, affordable place to live. In many neighborhoods, white families and real estate agents refused to rent or sell to Black people; in turn, the areas where Black people could find housing grew more and more rundown and overcrowded—which also drove up rents.

Starting in the 1930s, federal agencies like the Home Owners' Loan Corporation (HOLC) and the Federal Housing Authority wanted to increase homeownership among Americans. They wanted to ensure that banks would provide more people with home loans and give them a longer period of time to pay back those loans. So the HOLC developed a color-coded, A–D rating system where they assessed neighborhoods as more or less safe for investment. This would help banks feel good about making more investments. This rating system gave higher grades to white neighborhoods, which were seen as the safest and best for investment. And it rewarded new housing developments, so white people often had an easier time getting loans by moving into newly emerging suburbs rather than staying in the city. Home loans for Black people were scarce.

HOLC created maps rating neighborhoods for nearly 250 cities across the country. The best ratings (the letter A, color-coded green) were typically given to white neighborhoods with high quality housing still seen as prime for more housing and business development. The lowest rating (the letter D, color-coded red) was typically given to the neighborhoods with Black residents with older housing stock. The letter D was chosen because of the "infiltration of a lower-grade population," and the color red was assigned to show banks that these neighborhoods were "hazardous" for lending. The term "red-lining" is derived from this practice, because the areas on the map given D ratings, which banks were advised not to invest in, were outlined in red. This led to rundown properties in these neighborhoods because people also had difficulty obtaining loans to fix up their property. This also meant that no matter how much Black people had earned or saved, they found it incredibly difficult to get a home loan or find realtors willing to sell to them.

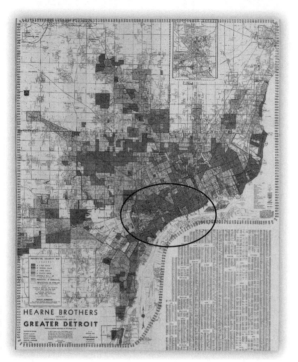

Detroit HOLC map. The government decided some neighborhoods were "unsafe" for investment.

Essentially, the federal government played a pivotal role in legitimizing and expanding Northern segregation. Detroit's growing suburbs were given high ratings, which spurred migration by white people; on the flip side, 50 percent of all city homes were "red-lined" and deemed unsafe for investment, even in solidly middle-class Black neighborhoods that had high-quality housing.

Housing segregation was also upheld by the use of restrictive covenants. These were provisions written into the house contract where the buyer of the home promised not to later sell it to a Black family. (Restrictive covenants were also used against Jewish families for many years.) And when some Black Detroiters managed to move into "white" neighborhoods, white Detroiters often rose up in anger and sometimes with violence.

In 1948, the Supreme Court took on the cases of four Black homeowners, including Detroit residents Orsel and Minnie McGhee, who challenged the use of these restrictive covenants. The

White Detroiters erected this sign in 1942 to protest Black people moving in to the Sojourner Truth Homes.

court ruled unanimously in *Shelley v. Kraemer* that courts could not enforce restrictive covenants because they violated the equal protection clause of the Fourteenth Amendment. (Restrictive covenants were so widespread that three Supreme Court justices removed themselves from hearing the case—likely due to such covenants on their own properties.)

But the Supreme Court decision did not *prohibit* the covenants—it just stopped courts from enforcing them. This left a loophole for homeowners, public officials, and real estate agents, who continued the practice. So Northern cities continued to be as segregated in 1960 as they'd been in 1940, partly because the Federal Housing Authority supported the division.

Despite the Black community's joy over the court's decision against restrictive covenants, Detroit housing authorities refused to honor it. Along with banks and realtors, they developed strategies to maintain these discriminatory practices—just as white officials and businesspeople were doing across the country. According to Detroit's NAACP executive secretary Arthur Johnson,

"Detroit newspapers wrote detailed articles instructing and encouraging white homeowners to circumvent the law and keep Blacks out. This was indicative of how the mainstream media in Detroit was but an extension of the white institutional power structure."

Between 1945 and 1955, about one hundred thousand private homes were built on vacant city land—but only 2 percent of these homes were available to Black people.

White people also had little trouble obtaining public housing apartments, while the waiting list for public housing in the Black community was six thousand deep. For many Black families, including the Parkses, finding a decent and affordable place to rent was exceedingly difficult. There were limited places to rent—and rents in Black neighborhoods continued to rise. And unlike in Montgomery, where the Parkses had lived in public housing, that option for Black families was scarce as well.

Rosa wrote many letters to Septima Clark at Highlander about the trouble her family was having: "rent is so expensive if a house is fit to live in."

But housing segregation wasn't the only problem. Detroit's schools were still deeply segregated. In 1962, *Ebony* magazine reported that 45 percent of Detroit's Black students went to schools that were more than 80 percent Black and that these schools often lacked the funding and resources of schools that served Detroit's white high schools. Not only that but the curriculum across the city was filled with racist stereotypes of Black people and contained almost no Black history or literature. In 1963, a group of students at Detroit's Northwestern High School launched a protest about the lack of Black history in the curriculum. Some teachers coldly responded, "Black people didn't do anything." Under this racist structure, Black students were often discouraged from attending college or skilled-trade programs.

Many public spaces were segregated as well. Several of Detroit's restaurants refused to serve Black people—though they didn't post signs about it, as happened in parts of the South. Detroit hospitals separated Black and white patients, and some even maintained segregated wards entirely. (The city's hospitals would not fully desegregate until the 1964 Civil Rights Act.) The Arcadia skating rink, which was centrally located downtown, didn't allow Black skaters to pass through its doors, and many businesses refused to hire Black people or only hired them for the most menial work.

The Parks family experienced a particularly difficult year in 1959. Work was scarce, and they burned through the $1,300 Rosa had saved from her job at Hampton. Rosa's niece recalled her aunt leaving the house in the morning "always neat as a pin" to look for work . . . with no success.

Raymond had struggled when they got to Detroit. Though he'd been a barber for more than twenty years in Alabama, barbers in Michigan were required to go to school and get a license before they could work. He got a maintenance job at the Michigan Barber School to help with this but then was laid off. Tax records show that he and Rosa made only $660 that year, which was incredibly low compared to the year of her bus arrest, when they were financially struggling but still recorded an income of $3,749. In April, they tried to buy a refrigerator at a warehouse sale, but they couldn't make the first payment, so the store took the fridge back.

The Parkses' income tax records, 1955 (before the boycott) and in 1959 (in Detroit).

Unable to afford the seventy-dollar monthly rent on their apartment, in July 1959, Rosa, Raymond, and Leona moved into a tiny, two-room apartment in the Progressive Civic League (PCL) building. Rosa and Raymond would serve as the building's caretakers, which reduced their rent to forty dollars a month. The PCL was made up of Black professionals, and it provided social services to the Black community, as well as some political advocacy. The social worker who hired Rosa and Raymond wrote a condescending letter to Rosa, instructing her "to have the folks who visit you come dressed neatly," as their neighbors had complained.

Both Rosa and Raymond were admitted to the hospital in the late 1950s; Raymond had been hospitalized for pneumonia in 1958, and, in December 1959, Rosa needed an operation for the ulcers that had been flaring up since the boycott. The Parkses didn't have health insurance, and the hospital bill cost $560 (more than their rent for the whole year!). They weren't able to pay, so the bill went to collections, which added more money in interest fees. Rosa and Raymond chipped away at it slowly, paying ten dollars each month.

The Parks family wasn't alone in the problems they were facing; many Black people who'd migrated to the North were also affected by the lack of affordable housing and health insurance, had difficulty affording food and other necessities, and struggled to get jobs. Rosa was proud. Just like back in Montgomery, she did not want to ask for help or even let people know about her struggles. But when she became particularly desperate, she was sometimes willing to tell people about her situation, perhaps in hopes that others would advocate on her behalf.

The Black press began to take notice of her situation. An article ran in the *Michigan Chronicle* in 1959 with the headline "Alabama Boycott Heroine Can't Find a Job!" They quoted Parks saying she and Raymond weren't sorry about the move but "work is hard to find" in Detroit. There had been no welcome wagon from Northern white liberals for Black activists fleeing Southern persecution.

In 1960, Rosa agreed to do an interview with *Jet*, a very popular Black magazine. That July, *Jet* published a hard-hitting article with the cover headline "The Bus Boycott's Forgotten Woman." The piece detailed her poverty and described her as a "tattered version of her former self—penniless, debt-ridden, ailing with stomach ulcers and a throat tumor, compressed into two rooms with her husband and mother."

The magazine also noted how Rosa had helped raise thousands of dollars for churches, the Montgomery Improvement Association (MIA), and the NAACP during the boycott. Still, she told the reporter, "If I had to do it all over again, I would still do it, even though I know what I know now."

Many Black people across the country were horrified. Some sent money or took up donations in their churches or other community groups. Black newspapers like the *Pittsburgh Courier* ran articles. Friends in Montgomery, along with the MIA, sent money. The donations and letters of support lifted the Parks family's spirits, but they were no replacement for steady work or decent housing.

Despite their difficult situation, Parks enjoyed the joys of family living close by. She regularly saw her cousins Thomas Williamson and Annie Cruse and their families, along with her brother, Sylvester (who was working at

Chrysler), his wife, Daisy, and their thirteen children. Sylvester's family lived in Southwest Detroit in a house with a huge garden, which Rosa liked to help tend. Since money was tight for both families, they grew a great deal of their own food, and Rosa would preserve food for the winter by canning. She was also a skilled cook. Her niece Sheila McCauley Keys remembered "little silver dollars of cornbread, griddle cakes, apple butter, fruit compote, chicken and dumplings." Her nieces also recalled that nothing was wasted; their aunt Rosa recycled everything. She sewed clothing for herself and her family. Her niece Rhea McCauley said, "I loved going over." So did her cousin Carolyn.

Throughout the myriad hardships that plagued her life in the North, Rosa Parks found comfort in her family.

# CHAPTER EIGHTEEN

# ROSA PARKS JOINS THE FIGHT UP NORTH

Once she'd returned from Hampton, Rosa Parks became politically active in her new home of Detroit. She might have been new in the city—and two decades of activism in Montgomery might have led some people to feel they'd done enough—but her activism didn't let up.

At first, she didn't join the local chapter of the NAACP; it seemed dominated by the interests of middle-class people and not as politically involved as she would have liked. Instead, Parks teamed up with the more radical Black union activists in the area. Many of the United Auto Workers Local 600 members, who'd brought her to Detroit during the boycott, became key sources of friendship and solidarity. This group included Louise Tappes, who was involved with the NAACP, served as president of the Women's Public Affairs Committee, and was the wife of United Auto Workers leader Sheldon

Tappes. Louise would become one of Rosa's close friends and travel companions.

Mrs. Parks also joined forces with more radical NAACP members, like those in the River Rouge chapter. Located next to Detroit, River Rouge was home to a massive Ford Motor Company auto plant. River Rouge's NAACP branch was filled with activist auto workers, including people who identified as Communists, or those who were not afraid to be associated with them. River Rouge's chapter was also more focused on activism, similar to how Parks and E. D. Nixon had run the Montgomery branch back in the 1940s, taking up a variety of political issues.

In 1959, the branch launched a boycott of the River Rouge Savings Bank when it refused to hire Black people. In 1960, it passed a resolution condemning the assassination of Patrice Lumumba, an independence leader who had become the first prime minister of the Congo. (Later, it was found that the CIA had played a role in Lumumba's assassination.) The national NAACP disapproved of the River Rouge chapter's actions, but Rosa Parks wholeheartedly supported its broad vision and commitment to direct action.

The president of the River Rouge branch, Lasker Smith, was horrified when the *Jet* article detailing Parks's financial troubles was published, and the group fundraised for her locally. Smith also reached out to the national NAACP office, trying to get them to help as well. The national office worried about bad publicity, as Parks had been such a strong supporter of the organization, which the article made clear. Gloster Current, the NAACP's director of branches, asked Smith to look into

Parks's job and health situation, and then told Smith to drive Parks to the airport to meet him when he came to town. Once there, Current told Parks that the organization was concerned with her family's welfare, but he scolded her for being so candid with *Jet*. Current wrote privately to NAACP head Roy Wilkins that "[Parks's] case may well plague us in the future."

Thanks to the efforts of Smith and his River Rouge chapter, in November 1960, nearly a year after Parks's hospitalization, the national NAACP office agreed to pay her hospital bill. Still, leaders instructed her not to talk to the media about such matters in the future.

After two years serving as caretakers at the Progressive Civic League building, in 1961, the Parks family was finally able to move. They rented the first floor of a house in the Virginia Park neighborhood, on the corner of Wildemere and Virginia Park, in what Parks described as the "heart of the ghetto." They would live there for fifteen years. Rosa had secured a job at the Stockton Sewing Company doing piecework, which meant she was paid according to how many pieces she sewed instead of at an hourly rate. The work was hard and exhausting.

Raymond had gotten his barber's license and was able to find work around the corner at the Wildemere Barber Shop. Vonzie Whitlow, who apprenticed for Raymond, recalled the barbershop was filled with discussion of everything from politics to baseball. Raymond would brag about his razor, saying "it could shave a baby's face."

Things were starting to look up. She thrilled to the younger people getting involved in Detroit's many Black movements—and Raymond often had people stopping by their new home or the barbershop to talk politics as well.

Organizing a new generation of freedom fighters in Detroit

Shortly after moving to Detroit, Rosa Parks found a
new church home at St. Matthew AME. Her cousin Annie
Cruse and friend Mary Hay Gaskins were members.
Parks attended every Sunday and often stopped by during
the week to pray or help out with other tasks. By 1965,
she had been promoted to deaconess, the highest position
a woman could attain at that time in the AME Church.

While St. Matthew was her church home, Rosa was
also drawn to activities at Reverend Albert Cleage's
Central United Church of Christ. Cleage's church held
numerous programs on the Black struggle and Black consciousness that interested her—and the church was close
to her Virginia Park home. The mix of Black militancy
and Christianity that developed in Detroit, particularly at
Cleage's church, resonated with her.

Reverend Cleage had grown up in Detroit, but he
left to attend Oberlin College in Ohio and the University

of Southern California. When he returned to Detroit, in 1954, he became pastor of St. Mark's Presbyterian Church. He felt stifled there after a while, though, and decided to found his own church, Central Congregational, which would later become Central United Church of Christ. Cleage also helped found an independent Black political party called the Freedom Now Party, in 1963, which spoke out against urban renewal, police brutality, and the lack of support for Black businesses in the city; ran candidates for public office; published a newspaper; and pushed for Black history in school curriculum. He became a leading Christian voice for Black nationalism in the coming years, and his church would serve as a key meeting and movement space. Parks would go there often and was an early supporter of the Freedom Now Party.

Her faith was central to her political courage. She had long believed that God stood with the oppressed and did not admire complacency. As Mississippi activist Fannie Lou Hamer said, "You can pray until you faint. But unless you get up and try to do something, God is not going to put it in your lap!" Mrs. Parks agreed.

Black Detroiters had protested the city's pervasive housing and school segregation, holding meetings and rallies, and picketing against it. But mostly they'd been ignored or disparaged by city leaders and white Detroiters. By 1963, the Black community had become frustrated with the lack of change. So civil rights leaders Reverend Cleage and Reverend C. L. Franklin called for a citywide march—a Great Walk for Freedom—to ensure that city leaders could no longer ignore this serious inequality. As Reverend Franklin told the *Detroit News*, the march would serve as a "warning to the city that what has transpired in the past is no longer acceptable to the Negro community."

On June 23, 1963, nearly two hundred thousand people dressed in their Sunday best—90 percent of them Black—marched through the heart of downtown Detroit. So many people filled the streets that local activist General Baker said of their trek up one of the city's busiest streets, "We didn't have to walk but were pushed up Jefferson."

Martin Luther King Jr. traveled to Detroit to take part in the march. Rosa Parks marched up front with him, but again, the media focused on King and the other local ministers. No one interviewed Parks that day, and many didn't even note her presence. At the end of the march, leaders including Reverend Cleage and Dr. King spoke candidly of the racism in Detroit, calling on those gathered to keep fighting the city's racial injustice and segregation.

Parks thought King's speech was the best she'd ever heard him give, "reminding everybody that segregation and discrimination were rampant in Michigan as well as Alabama." Motown put out a record album of Dr. King's speech, and she played it over and over.

King's speech that day was a preview of the themes he would preach at the March on Washington for Jobs and Freedom, just two months later: "I have a dream this afternoon that one day right here in Detroit, Negroes will be able to buy a house or rent a house anywhere that their money will carry them, and they will be able to get a job."

■  ■  ■

Meanwhile, the movement down South had heated up as well. Downtown department stores, one of the main places people shopped, were willing to sell their goods to Black people, but they didn't let Black people actually eat in their restaurants or try on their clothes before buying. This was a widespread problem and angered many Black people, who were tired of these stores taking their money but not serving them equally.

Black students took the lead. Four freshmen at a Black college called North Carolina A&T, in Greensboro, became fed up with hearing people *talk* about the need for change. So, on February 1, 1960, they decided to do something about it.

That afternoon, Joseph McNeil, Ezell Blair, Franklin McCain, and David Richmond went to one of these stores, called Woolworth's, bought some school supplies (which proved the store was willing to take their money), then sat down at the lunch counter and asked to be served. Flustered, the lunch counter staff refused.

So, the young men kept sitting there. They'd vowed they would continue silently protesting until the lunch counter was desegregated.

Woolworth's closed the counter for the day, thinking the young men would get tired and move on to a new cause.

However, when they returned to campus, word had spread about their action. And, the next day, when the young men went back to the Woolworth's lunch counter, they were joined by *twenty-three* more students, including young women from nearby Bennett College who were also organizing against segregation. The day after that, *sixty-three* students took part. On the fourth day, the numbers of students sitting in continued to grow, and three white students joined the sit-ins. But white thugs attacked the protestors. And by that Saturday, more than *three hundred people* were sitting at the lunch counters at Woolworth's and the nearby Kress department store in Greensboro.

Inspired by this nonviolent protest, other Black students in other cities saw that they, too, could do what the Greensboro students were doing, and they began sitting in themselves at downtown lunch counters and other stores that didn't treat Black people equally. By the next week, sit-ins were launched in the Southern cities of Charlotte, Raleigh, and Hampton, eventually spreading to Nashville and Chattanooga, Tennessee; Orangeburg, South Carolina; and Rosa Parks's old home of Montgomery. The sit-ins continued to spread to dozens more Southern cities and towns over the next few months. Sympathy protests took place outside Woolworth's in Northern cities as well. The vast majority of students sitting in were Black, but some white students joined as well.

At first, city leaders and business owners tried to ignore the protestors, expecting them to get bored and leave. But they kept coming back. They often came dressed up, determined to project a proud, dignified image, and many times, they brought their homework to do at the sit-ins.

When the protestors didn't give up, cities began arresting them. Angry white people attacked, hitting them, dumping food on them, shoving them around. And the police rarely arrested these white attackers.

But these young people refused to move—and they didn't strike back. When they were arrested, others took their places. And they kept returning, often bringing more people with them the next day.

Between February 1960 and February 1962, sit-ins took place in more than 150 cities. And, ultimately, thousands of lunch counters and other facilities in these 150 Southern cities were integrated as a result.

More than seven thousand people went to jail, and more than one hundred thousand people had actively participated in this new movement. The sit-ins showed the power of young people to move the civil rights struggle forward. They combined nonviolence with confrontation, showing the world that a new generation would not stand for business as usual.

Many white Southerners seemed surprised by the anger and disruption. They'd long preferred to think that Black people were content with their place in America, and they certainly didn't like what they believed was unreasonable and unnecessary behavior. However, the sit-ins soon debunked this self-deception.

Some older Black leaders were also critical of the sit-ins and did not approve. They feared what would happen to the young people involved and didn't believe such confrontational strategies were a wise way to push for change. This meant that many sit-in participants were going against the wishes of their families and colleges. Some schools even suspended students who took part in the sit-ins or put them on probation. Parents were angry, too, and people like Spelman College student Gwen Robinson (later Zoharah Simmons) had to deal with their families instructing them not to get involved. Getting arrested was a badge of shame—plus it was incredibly dangerous. But Simmons, like many others, did not follow her parents' wishes.

Rosa Parks's organizer friend Ella Baker was delighted. Baker loved the bold spirit these young organizers showed and didn't want that diminished or co-opted by existing civil rights groups. She had recently moved to Atlanta because she had been hired to get the SCLC's Crusade for Citizenship off the ground and was serving as acting executive director of the organization. Seeing the need for these young people to meet one another, Baker planned a conference to bring them together. From April 16 to 18, 1960, at Baker's alma mater Shaw University, more than 120 students from fifty-six colleges and high schools in twelve Southern states and Washington, DC, gathered to talk about the protests and figure out what could come next.

Baker mentored the young activists, pushing to make sure they created their own organization, charted their own path, and did not get swallowed up into existing civil rights groups. As she had impressed upon Parks fifteen years earlier in those NAACP workshops, Baker believed in people's ability to lead and organize themselves. And Baker brought this same message to these young organizers.

What came out of this meeting was the Student Nonviolent Coordinating Committee, or SNCC. The organization believed in the power of nonviolence and the ability of ordinary people to effectively lead themselves. With young people at the helm, SNCC was one of the boldest civil rights organizations of the time. Over the next few years, the young people of SNCC would take the movement forward across the South. Most of the students leading SNCC were Black, but there were white students involved from the start as well.

Rosa Parks was thrilled by this movement. She had long believed that young people would lead the way to change—and here again, they were blazing a trail and pulling the adults in their communities along with them. She met a number of the student activists during trips she made back to Highlander Folk School and praised their efforts. As she noted to a reporter, it was young people who were keeping the civil rights movement going. These younger activists were encouraged by her support, and, according to SNCC's Martha Norman Noonan, knew "how much she was with us."

# CHAPTER NINETEEN

# THE MARCH ON WASHINGTON FOR JOBS AND FREEDOM

The idea for the March on Washington for Jobs and Freedom in 1963 began as a way to call attention to the one hundredth anniversary of the Emancipation Proclamation. A *century* after the end of slavery, Black people were still not free.

So, labor leaders A. Philip Randolph and Bayard Rustin devised the march as a protest for "jobs and justice." Originally their plans included massive civil disobedience in Washington, DC. But Randolph and Rustin wanted to build a coalition of *all* the major civil rights groups—from the Student Nonviolent Coordinating Committee and Southern Christian Leadership Conference to more moderate groups like the Urban League and NAACP, which frowned upon civil disobedience.

The sole woman on the march coordinating committee was longtime Black activist Anna Arnold Hedgeman. Hedgeman had worked for the federal government's Fair Employment Practices Commission, served as dean at Howard University, and then took a job on the Commission of Race and Religion for the National Council of Churches. Through her work with the National Council of Churches, Hedgeman helped bring many white Christians, including white clergy, into the civil rights struggle. The March on Washington would be the first mass civil rights event with large numbers of white people; they were estimated to have made up 25 percent of the marchers. Hedgeman also facilitated many of the day's logistics, including Operation Sandwich, in which she commanded a huge volunteer group to produce eighty thousand box lunches for the marchers.

From its beginning, women were marginalized when it came to planning the march. Hedgeman grew increasingly frustrated and pushed for the inclusion of more women on the organizing committee and in the program itself. No women were slated to speak. National Council of Negro Women (NCNW) president Dorothy Height was not given a formal role nor was she was included in descriptions of the march leadership. This was so despite the fact that the NCNW had fundraised for the protest and Height had been meeting with the other leaders for months as part of an initiative to coordinate activities and fundraising among the major civil rights groups.

Height and Hedgeman pressed for women's inclusion, but according to Height, march co-organizer Bayard Rustin responded, "Women are included. Every group has women in it." Height later observed, "Clearly there was a low tolerance level for anyone raising the questions about the women's participation."

Angered by this absence, civil rights lawyer Pauli Murray wrote to march co-organizer A. Philip Randolph:

> I have been increasingly perturbed over the blatant
> disparity between the major role which Negro women
> have played and are playing in the crucial grass-roots
> levels of our struggle and the minor role of leadership
> they have been assigned in the national policy-making
> decisions. . . . The time has come to say to you quite
> candidly, Mr. Randolph, that "tokenism" is as offensive
> when applied to women as when applied to Negroes.

Hedgeman continued to object as well, asserting the march should actually be called "Rosa Parks Day" since Parks had been the one to start what became a national movement.

But their valid criticisms were treated as inappropriate and counterproductive to the protest. Finally, Randolph and Rustin proposed a compromise: the program would include a tribute to women in which a select group of women would stand up and be recognized by the crowd. The six they chose were Rosa Parks, Gloria Richardson (leader of the movement in Cambridge, Maryland), Diane Nash (one of SNCC's founders), Myrlie Evers (wife of slain NAACP leader Medgar Evers), Prince Lee (wife of slain voting rights activist Herbert Lee), and Daisy Bates (the head of Arkansas's NAACP). However, no woman would be allowed to formally address the attendees.

On August 28, 1963, nearly a quarter of a million people arrived in Washington, DC, to demand civil rights, jobs, and justice. The city prepared for the march as if it were expecting a military battle. Law enforcement from local police to the FBI monitored the protest intensively under code name Operation Steep Hill. They even installed a kill-switch in the microphone. All elective surgeries in the city were canceled, and all liquor stores were closed.

People made the journey to DC via trains, buses, vans, and cars. Rustin had planned everything down to a tee: from having lunches for marchers to bathrooms to places for the buses to park. People arrived bearing signs that detailed the struggles they'd been waging at home in places such as Philadelphia, Chicago, Harlem, Birmingham, Little Rock, Los Angeles, and Greensboro:

> WE DEMAND AN END TO POLICE BRUTALITY
> WE MARCH FOR INTEGRATED SCHOOLS NOW
> WE MARCH FOR HIGHER MINIMUM WAGES,
> COVERAGE FOR ALL WORKERS NOW
> FREEDOM NOW

Waves and waves of people filled the park space between the Lincoln Memorial and the Washington Monument. Washington had never seen anything like this.

The main march, led by A. Philip Randolph, with Dr. King and others a few paces behind, progressed down Constitution Avenue to the Lincoln Memorial. The wives of the leaders were not allowed to march with their husbands. Instead, the women to be honored that day led a small, separate side march. Gloria Richardson recalled the NAACP calling her ahead of time and instructing her to wear a hat, gloves, and a dress rather than jeans. Richardson did not appreciate the dress code, so she scoured the Eastern Shore of Maryland until she found a jeans skirt to wear.

People came to the March on Washington from all over the country.

The march was followed by a full program of speakers. Parks, Bates, Richardson, and Lee sat silently on the dais. (Myrlie Evers and Diane Nash were not present.) Bates, who led the Arkansas NAACP through the desegregation of Central High School in 1957, introduced the Tribute to Women—a 142-word introduction written by NAACP aide John Morsell that pledged the continued role of women in struggle for civil rights. Bates began by saying, "Mr. Randolph, the women of this country pledge to you, Mr. Randolph, to Martin Luther King, to Roy Wilkins and all of you fighting for civil liberties, that we will join hands with you, as women of this country."

This meant the only words spoken by a woman during the formal program of the march were written for her and contained a pledge to support the men of the movement, despite the fact that the women on the dais and in the crowd that day had risked their lives for years—decades, for some—to push for civil rights.

Randolph seemed flustered during this portion of the program, and at one point he forgot which women were actually being recognized! "Uh, who else?" he said. "Will the . . ."

Someone on the dais said, "Rosa Parks."

"Miss Rosa Parks," Randolph continued. "Will they all stand."

Parks stood and offered eight words of acknowledgment: "Hello, friends of freedom; it's a wonderful day." Richardson managed to get out a "hello" before the microphone was taken from her.

Hedgeman, who was also sitting on the dais that day, described the feeling of listening to the tribute: "We grinned; some of us as we recognized anew that Negro women are second-class citizens in the same way that white women are in our culture." Rosa Parks was dumbfounded that the world-famous dancer-actress Josephine Baker, who'd also been on the dais that day, was not allowed to speak. Parks told Daisy Bates that afternoon that she hoped for a "better day coming."

Famous singers Bob Dylan, Joan Baez, Marian Anderson, and Mahalia Jackson all performed at the march. And there were many speeches. Randolph gave the opening remarks. The NAACP's Roy Wilkins, labor leader Walter Reuther, American Jewish Council president Joachim Prinz, and leader of the Congress of Racial Equality (CORE) Floyd McKissick all spoke. So did SNCC's chair, John Lewis, although he was pressured to edit his speech so that it would be less controversial. SNCC's politics were often bolder than those of other civil rights groups, and this made many older leaders uncomfortable. The youngest speaker at the march, Lewis, had to remove criticisms of President John F. Kennedy's civil rights bill as "too little and too late," the word "revolution," and the question "Which side is the federal government on?" But it was still one of the day's hardest-hitting speeches.

At the March on Washington

Then Dr. King gave a breathtaking speech. Television stations aired it live, and for many white Americans, including President Kennedy himself, this was probably the first time they'd heard a full-length speech or sermon by a Black person.

While King's speech is now one of the most celebrated in American history, it is largely known for its "I have a dream" ending. Many forget the beginning, in which King laid out how America had given Black people a "bad check." He said the country had "defaulted on this promissory note insofar as her citizens of color are concerned," so the protestors had come to Washington to collect on a debt stemming from generations of exploitation of Black labor. King's vision at the march was that the nation had a debt to Black people, and that Black people had come to claim their rightful payment. The day wasn't all about dreaming—in reality, it was about guaranteed civil rights and long-overdue compensation.

Just before King was about to speak, Gloria Richardson was hustled into a cab, along with famous actress-singer Lena Horne, and sent back to the hotel where they were staying. The march organizers claimed they were worried the two women would get crushed in the mob of people. But no one else was sent back to the hotel.

"They did this," Richardson believed, "because Lena Horne had had Rosa Parks by the hand and had been taking her to satellite broadcasts, saying, 'This is who started the civil rights movement, not Martin Luther King. This is the woman you need to interview.'" Richardson had helped Horne bring reporters from various international news agencies to Parks. "We got several people to interview Rosa Parks. The March organizers must have found that out."

After the march, ten civil rights leaders met with President Kennedy—but no women were allowed to come. Dorothy Height observed, "I've never seen a more immovable force. We could not get women's participation taken seriously." Anna Arnold Hedgeman was indignant that Parks, not to mention any of the other women responsible for the movement's success, wasn't invited.

Awed by the assembled crowd, Hedgeman reflected that "in front of 250,000 people who had come to Washington because they had a dream, and in the face of all the men and women of the past who had dreamed in vain, I wished very much that Martin had said, 'We have a dream.'"

Today, the March on Washington is seen as one of the most American events of the twentieth century. But at the time, most Americans did not view it that way. Just before the March on Washington, a Gallup poll found that only 23 percent of Americans favored the proposed

Do you think "sit-ins" at lunch counters, "Freedom Buses" and other demonstrations by Negroes will hurt or help the Negro's chances of being integrated in the South?

| | |
|---|---|
| Hurt | 57% |
| Help | 27% |
| No opinion | 15% |

**GALLUP, MAY 28 – JUNE 2, 1961**

Do you think mass demonstrations by Negroes are more likely to HELP or more likely to HURT the Negro's cause for racial equality?

| | JUNE 1963 | MAY 1964 |
|---|---|---|
| Help | 27% | 16% |
| Hurt | 60% | 74% |
| Make no difference | 4% | 4% |
| No opinion | 9% | 6% |

**GALLUP, 1963 and 1964**

Gallup polls showed most Americans didn't support the civil rights movement.

civil rights demonstration. Most people did not approve of the march, and many congressmen attacked it as mob rule and "un-American."

Before the march, Senator Strom Thurmond took to the floor of the US Senate, using information provided to him from the FBI, to attack march organizer Bayard Rustin. Rustin was gay. He had also refused to serve in World War II in a segregated army. Thurmond called him a "Communist, draft dodger, and homosexual," hoping it would cause backlash against the march. It didn't work—civil rights leaders knew Thurmond's segregationist views and, even though some were homophobic themselves, they rallied to support Rustin.

In the 1960s, the vast majority of white people disapproved of the civil rights movement and its tactics. In May 1961, a Gallup survey revealed that only 22 percent of Americans approved of the Freedom Riders (the Freedom Riders had ridden buses through the South, encountering tremendous violence, to pressure the federal government to enforce its own law that interstate buses had to be desegregated), and 57 percent said the "sit-ins at lunch counters, freedom buses, and other demonstrations by Negroes were hurting the Negro's chances of being integrated in the South." This wasn't just a Southern phenomenon; in 1964, the *New York Times* revealed that 57 percent of New Yorkers thought the civil rights movement had gone too far.

The FBI had taken notice of Dr. King and had been monitoring the civil rights movement for a while. FBI director J. Edgar Hoover found King and many of the movements' activities suspicious. After King's speech at the March on Washington, the FBI—with the approval of the Kennedy administration—decided to increase its surveillance of the civil rights leader. The FBI described King as "the most dangerous [person] . . . to the Nation . . . from the standpoint . . . of national security." And Attorney General Robert F. Kennedy signed off on the FBI's request to surveil Dr. King, bugging and wiretapping his home, office, phones, and hotel rooms, as well as those of his associates. That meant everywhere he went, from his home to his church to every hotel room he stayed in, the government was recording what he was saying. The government was suspicious of the growing influence of the civil rights movement—and of King in particular.

# CHAPTER TWENTY

# WORKING FOR JOHN CONYERS

**R**osa Parks continued her political work after the March on Washington—and there was still plenty to do.

Black people in Michigan were able to register and vote in Michigan, unlike in Montgomery. But they faced another barrier, and that was how the districts were drawn. Gerrymandering is the process of drawing districts to dilute the voting power of certain groups, to favor a certain political party or a certain group of people. So, although Black people were voting, their votes were spread over many districts, which meant they couldn't elect people to represent their interests.

In 1962, the Supreme Court ruled in the case *Baker v. Carr* that the way districts were drawn disadvantaged urban voters, particularly Black voters. So voting districts were redrawn across the country to provide more equitable political representation to urban Black communities. Two years later, in 1964,

Michigan's redrawn First Congressional District meant
that the state would likely send a second Black person
to Congress. (Congressman Charles Diggs already represented Michigan's Thirteenth District.)

The field was crowded with candidates, and a Black
Democratic accountant named Richard Austin was the favored one. Rosa Parks decided to volunteer on what was
considered a long-shot campaign, that of a radical young
civil rights lawyer named John Conyers.

Born in Highland Park, Michigan, thirty-five-year-old
Conyers had been educated in Detroit's public school
system and attended Wayne State University, where he
obtained his undergraduate and law degrees. He served
in the army during the Korean War. In 1963, he'd gone
to Alabama as a legal observer around voter registration,
and he was known in the civil rights circles Parks traveled in. Conyers was a fierce supporter of unions and an
early opponent of the United States' involvement in the
Vietnam War, as was Rosa Parks. He ran on a "jobs, justice, and peace" platform and received support from the
emerging antiwar movement, civil rights advocates, and
portions of Detroit's labor movement.

Mrs. Parks began attending campaign meetings, rarely
speaking up but willing to help with whatever campaign
tasks needed doing. "Everyone was frozen in their tracks,"
Conyers recalled. "Rosa Parks is supporting Conyers."

In April 1964, she helped persuade Martin Luther
King Jr. to come to Detroit to do an event with Conyers.
King had been avoiding political races and endorsements,
but he couldn't say no to Mrs. Parks. Conyers felt that
King's support increased his visibility in the city. "If it

wasn't for Rosa Parks," he said, "I never would have gotten elected." The primary election was exceedingly close, with eight candidates vying for the Democratic nomination. It went to a recount, and in the end, Conyers won the primary by about forty votes. In November 1964, he beat Republican Robert Blackwell and was elected to Congress.

During this time, the Parks family was doing better financially than they had been in the past, but they were still facing difficulties. Rosa's job at the Stockton Sewing Company was hard—in many ways, the place was a glorified sweatshop—but it was full-time work. And Raymond was still working at the Wildemere Barber Shop around the corner from their Virginia Park apartment. They had no health insurance.

Knowing how many long, hard years Rosa Parks had committed to helping the Black community, her Detroit friends organized a fundraiser for her. As a Women's Political Action Committee newsletter explained: "She has received many, many plaques and awards of merits, etc., from citizens all over the country, but as meritorious as they are, they do not compensate for Mrs. Parks having to move away from her home for fear of loss of her life, and neither do they compensate for the great financial loss of adequate income." On April 3, 1965, Coretta Scott King and Ralph Abernathy traveled to Detroit to join local ministers, women's groups, and labor leaders to honor "a woman of bold and audacious courage." Mrs. Parks received a thunderous standing ovation from the thousand people gathered at Cobo Hall, a huge auditorium in downtown Detroit.

Recognizing her skill, determination, and work for his campaign, one of the first things Conyers did when he took office in 1965 was hire Parks to work with constituents in his Detroit office. This was her first paid political position after more than twenty years of such work. It wasn't a huge salary, but it helped stabilize the Parks family's situation, particularly because the job came with health insurance. It was only after a year of working for Conyers that the Parks family was able to generate an income comparable to what they'd been making before her bus arrest—though that wasn't a large amount to begin with.

Conyers spent much of his time in Washington, DC, so Parks helped with daily operations and community issues back in Detroit. In her first years working for the congressman, she traveled all over the city, visiting constituents at schools, hospitals, and senior citizens homes; attending community meetings, union events, and rallies; and keeping Conyers grounded in community activism. Taking up various urban social issues, Parks gathered information about people's concerns and filled in for Conyers at public functions. Her job often focused on trying to address the inequalities Black Detroit residents were facing, particularly around unequal education, job discrimination, denial of Social Security or welfare benefits, and the need for more affordable housing. Prisoners would write to Parks, and she'd try to secure more fair treatment when possible.

Conyers aide Larry Horwitz said of Conyers and Parks's partnership: "She was a presence. John gave her a job and economic security. She gave John prestige and

Rosa Parks and John Conyers at a newspaper strike rally

stature. When he was very junior, after a bitterly divided
primary, he needed this." Parks was well-known and
respected in the Black community, but "there was an ab-
solute racial divide," Horwitz noted. "She was a heroine
in the Black community, but not the white community [at
that point]." Most white people who came to the office
in the early years didn't know who she was. Parks called
her varied and important work for Conyers "one of the
highlights of my life."

Parks also traveled with Conyers to national Black
events and to support Black candidates. Conyers aides
Horwitz and Leon Atchison made clear in later interviews, however, that Mrs. Parks made her own political
agenda, and that she attended many Black political events
because of her own beliefs and moral compass—not

because the congressman had sent her. In fact, she was traveling so much that at one point, she decided to have a conversation with the congressman, that perhaps he should lower her pay. Conyers was flabbergasted. It was "the only wage reduction conversation [he'd] ever had" with any staff member in his career, he said. He told Parks absolutely not, that the work she was doing around the country was uplifting his work.

As she grew older, and particularly after Raymond died in 1977, her position would become more ceremonial, greeting the many people who visited the office and meeting with groups, particularly schoolchildren. But in those early years, she was a key representative and community advocate for Conyers in the city.

Over the years, many journalists and historians came to interview Mrs. Parks in Detroit, often at Conyers's office. Yet most only wanted to talk about her life and work in Montgomery—and asked few questions about her work for Conyers or her experience of racism in Detroit. Many made assumptions that her activism was long since over. These assumptions were also tinged with sexism; it's hard to imagine a reporter interviewing a male civil rights activist from the South turned congressional aide and not asking him about the congressman's agenda or the most pressing issues facing Detroit. But that's exactly what they did with Parks.

One interviewer questioned her decision to leave the South and her civil rights work in the North. Parks pushed back: "I don't know whether I could have been more effective as a worker for freedom in the South than I am here in Detroit. Really, the same thing that has occurred in the South is existing here to a certain degree. We do have the same problems." The reporter didn't follow up. When interviewed on the tenth anniversary of the bus boycott, Parks told a reporter, "I can't say we like Detroit any better than Montgomery." But no one cared to probe that response.

When another journalist claimed that Parks had chosen not to participate in the Detroit civil rights movement, Parks pushed back yet again, saying she was playing a similar role in Detroit as she had in Montgomery: "I worked quietly and tried to do whatever I could in the community without projecting myself. And as far as I am concerned, I haven't changed. I'm just the same as I was in Montgomery." The lack of interest in her focus on fighting Northern racism meant that the second half of her life was largely hidden in plain sight.

Many white people were offended when Conyers hired her. The office was bombarded with hate mail and death threats, saying he'd hired a traitor and a "troublemaker." People sent all kinds of horrible things to the office, expressing their displeasure: rotten watermelons, voodoo dolls, and hateful cards and letters. Many callers were "quite threatening," but, according to Conyers's aide Leon Atchison, Parks would listen and simply tell them to "have a nice day." "She was cool—and didn't seem stressed about it."

A letter from May 19, 1969, complained: "We don't think John Conyers should be hiring a person of your low caliber, Rosa, to work in his office. Maybe in his private home for [the] purpose of scrubbing the floors as a domestic maid, perhaps—but certainly not doing office work. . . . John Conyers is a bad enough senator [sic] as

```
                                          Detroit, Mich.
                                          May 19,1969

Rosa Parks: --

     We don't think John Conyers should be hiring a person of your low
calibre Rosa,to work in his office. Maybe in his private home for pur-
pose of scrubbing the floors as a domestic maid ,perhaps - but certainly
not doing office work.

     You are far too much of a troublemaker and rabblerouser.We cannot
so soon forget all the chaos you made about "going to the back of the
bus". As a matter of fact,you are to blame gal,for the current revolu-
tion going on among the niggers and whites today! You ought to hang
that kinky ole haid of yours in deep shame gal for what you did!!

     John Conyers is a bad enough senator as it is,without his adding
fuel to the fire by hiring an evil dame in his office to help him.
Your two brains probably dig up plenty of bad ideas to bug us lawabiding
serious minded hardworking taxpayers. Frankly, we think you are strictly
good for nothing. That's why we would like to see all the nigs go back
to Africa and start a new homestead. Experience has taught you surely
that your presence in this country simply isn't working out satisfactor-
ily, so why don't you wise up and try something else for a change?
Instead of becoming better liked,negroes are rapidly becoming more and
more violently despised day after day,due to the crime they cause.
                                              Bratson
```

Hate letters streamed into Conyers's office
around his decision to hire Rosa Parks.

it is, without his adding fuel to the fire by hiring an evil
dame in his office to help him."

And a 1972 letter also clearly objected to her work in
Detroit, saying: "Why didn't you stay down South? The
North sure doesn't want you up here. You are the biggest
woman troublemaker ever."

So, fifteen years after she'd forged a historic resistance
to Southern segregation on the bus, many people objected
to Rosa Parks's important work in the North.

# CHAPTER TWENTY-ONE

# MEETING MALCOLM X

After the success of the Great Walk for Freedom, Detroit's civil rights ministers wanted to organize a group to take on Northern injustice.

Similar to Montgomery, postwar Detroit was home to a handful of politically active Black ministers who challenged the complacency of their white and Black peers. Many Black ministers had ties with the auto industry, and Black people wanting to work for an auto company usually had to get a letter from a minister attesting to their good character. In turn, these ministers were rewarded with gifts and well-paid congregants and, because of this, often didn't speak out on matters of civil rights. Ministers like C. L. Franklin, Horace White, Charles Hill, and Albert Cleage set out to break this tradition when they organized the Northern branch of Dr. King's Southern Christian Leadership Conference.

The ministers wanted to hold an event to kick off the Northern Christian Leadership Conference, but political differences soon emerged. Reverend Cleage wanted to invite Malcolm X, but the other ministers objected. So Cleage left the group and organized a separate group, the Grassroots Leadership Conference. Rosa Parks attended both.

Malcolm Little (who would later take the name Malcolm X) was born in 1925 in Nebraska. His father, Earl Little, was a minister and supporter of Marcus Garvey, just like Rosa's grandfather had been. The Little family moved to Lansing, Michigan, where Earl was run over by a streetcar and died. He was likely killed by white racists who were threatened by his work, but his death was ruled a suicide so that his family could not collect the life insurance. This thrust them deep into poverty.

Malcolm was a brilliant student, but when a teacher told him that his goal of becoming a lawyer was unrealistic for Black people—and that he should become a carpenter instead—he became disillusioned and ultimately dropped out. He started gambling and stealing to make ends meet. In 1946, he was arrested for burglary and sentenced to eight years in prison. While he was imprisoned, he read everything he could get his hands on, turning prison into a school for himself.

He was also introduced to the teachings of Elijah Muhammad and the Nation of Islam (NOI), a combination of the Muslim faith and Black nationalist capitalism. The NOI saw itself as working toward the spiritual, moral, and financial uplift of Black people, and some of its main goals were building independent Black businesses; encouraging moral purity; advocating racial separatism and self-defense; and anointing African Americans as the chosen people. Malcolm X joined the NOI, converting to Islam.

When he was released from prison in 1952, he was key to helping the Nation of Islam grow, rising quickly through the ranks to eventually head Mosque #7 in Harlem. His talents as a speaker and organizer helped the NOI's membership expand substantially. He also started the newspaper *Muhammad Speaks*, recognizing the power of having their own publication to cover different kinds of issues than the mainstream media did. NOI members sold copies on street corners, which built discipline and group solidarity.

Over time, though, Malcolm X grew disillusioned with Elijah Muhammad and the NOI. Malcolm wanted to be more politically active, and Muhammad was holding him back. In 1962, the secretary of the Los Angeles mosque was killed by the police, and Malcolm X traveled to the city to join in building a movement to challenge police brutality (and perhaps retaliate against the officer). He spoke in churches and connected with local civil rights activists who had been highlighting police abuse in Los Angeles for years. But Elijah Muhammad did not approve and told him to come home.

The leader of the NOI had started to become jealous of Malcolm X's popularity—and Malcolm X didn't like how Elijah Muhammad failed to follow his own moral teachings, having numerous children out of marriage and not supporting them.

Malcolm X's highly political speech in Detroit, which would come to be known as "Message to the Grass-roots," signaled to people like Gloria Richardson—who was in attendance and who he praised in the speech—that he was distancing himself from the NOI. Malcolm highlighted the need for Black people to stick together, forming a united front to attack racism. He pointed out the distinctions between the experiences of the "house Negro" and "field Negro":

> The house Negro usually lived close to his master. He dressed like his master. He wore his master's second-hand clothes. He ate food that his master left on the table. And he lived in his master's house—probably in the basement or the attic—but he still lived in the master's house. . . . His master's pain was his pain. And it hurt him more for his master to be sick than for him to be sick himself. When the house started burning down, that type of Negro would fight harder to put the master's house out than the master himself would.
>
> But then you had another Negro out in the field. The house Negro was in the minority. The masses—the field Negroes were the masses. If [the master's] house caught on fire, they'd pray for a wind to come along and fan the breeze. If someone came to the house Negro and said, "Let's go, let's separate," naturally that Uncle Tom would say, "Go where? What could I do without boss? Where would I live? . . . Who would look out for me?" That's the house Negro. But if you went to the field Negro and said, "Let's go, let's separate," he wouldn't even ask you where or how. He'd say, "Yes, let's go." . . . So now you have a twentieth-century type of house Negro. . . . He hasn't got anybody to defend him, but anytime you say "we" he says "we." "Our president," "our government."

Rosa and Raymond, like many of their friends, had been following Malcolm X's work for years.

According to one of his close political associates, Peter Bailey, Malcolm X had been extremely inspired by and spoke often about two civil rights activists: Rosa Parks and Mississippi voting rights activist Fannie Lou Hamer. He put out the word through friends that he wanted to meet Rosa Parks when he came to Detroit. And meet they did—in November 1963.

Three weeks later, Elijah Muhammad silenced Malcolm X for ninety days, after Malcolm had referred to President Kennedy's assassination as the "chickens coming home to roost." Malcolm argued that the violence America had sewn against people of color and other political leaders around the world and at home was coming back upon itself.

Malcolm split from the Nation of Islam permanently a few months later. He then founded his own political group, the Organization of Afro-American Unity, which was modeled on the pan-African group the Organization of African Unity, as well as a mosque called the Muslim Mosque. He returned to Detroit in April 1964 to give his "Ballot or the Bullet" speech, which Rosa Parks attended. There, Malcolm called on Black people to use their (voting) ballot independently and in unity to support Black interests. "It's time now for you and me to become more politically mature and realize what the ballot is for . . . and that if we don't cast a ballot, it's going to end up in a situation where we're going to have to cast a bullet. It's either a ballot or a bullet."

The last time Rosa Parks and Malcolm X met was a week before his assassination. The Afro-American Broadcasting Company was hosting an event with Malcolm as the keynote speaker and presenting Parks with an "Overdue" award. The Afro-American Broadcasting Company was formed to counter negative images of Black people in the media and in popular culture. The station hosted a two-hour radio program on Saturdays, which often featured Malcolm's speeches. And even though his house in Queens, New York, had just been bombed, Malcolm X made the trip. He and Mrs. Parks spoke the longest they ever had that evening, and she asked him to sign her program.

Activists needed other activists to get the work done, but they also needed them for support and inspiration to keep their courage up. Mrs. Parks had long drawn sustenance from her friends and fellow activists in the struggle. This was apparent in the relationship between Rosa Parks and Malcolm X as well. Full of conviction and pride, Malcolm reminded Parks of her grandfather—and his commitment to self-defense. Rosa also appreciated his boldness and clarity and his skill at getting to the heart of the liberal Northern racism she was experiencing in Detroit. Malcolm described Southern racism as the wolf and Northern racism as the fox, zeroing in on how Northerners claimed to be open minded and liberal but discriminated against Black people in jobs, schools, and housing nonetheless. Mrs. Parks saw him as "brilliant" and read all she could on his ministry and political program. But this was a mutual admiration society, as Malcolm was deeply inspired by her courage and perseverance and drew strength from her as well.

Like Malcolm X, Parks was also a lifelong believer in self-defense and didn't see a conflict between supporting organized nonviolence and the personal right to defend oneself: "I couldn't accept being pushed even at the cost

Admiring a poster
of Malcolm X at the
1972 Gary convention

of my life." She found nonviolent direct action like the
bus boycott "refreshing" and "more successful" than "if
violence had been used." Still, she found it "hard to say
that she was completely converted to it." In other words,
she saw the power and necessity in both methods.

To Rosa Parks, there was no contradiction between
her deep admiration for Malcolm X and her equally deep
admiration for Dr. Martin Luther King. She loved and respected them both—along with Ella Baker, Septima Clark,
Thurgood Marshall, Audley Moore (who became known

as Queen Mother Moore), Stokely Carmichael, and many, many others. Today, the civil rights and Black Power movements are often portrayed to be in opposition with each other, when in reality, many people like Parks saw them as related and intertwined—and took part in both.

For Rosa Parks, many of the key tenets of Black Power were ones she had long believed in and championed for decades:

- Independent Black political power
- The right to self-defense
- Fighting against police brutality
- Questioning unjust American foreign policy
- Supporting public assistance and antipoverty action
- Pushing for more Black history for all ages in all courses in every school

Her lifetime of political work ran the gamut when it came to approaches, and to her—as it was with Malcolm X—a Black united front was the key to moving forward in the Black struggle.

Rosa Parks would later refer to Malcolm X as her hero.

# CHAPTER TWENTY-TWO

# GOING (BACK) DOWN SOUTH

Just as Parks and Nixon had done in Montgomery, activists across the South saw the Black vote as key to dismantling racism in the South and enabling Black self-determination. The Student Nonviolent Coordinating Committee (SNCC) and the Southern Christian Leadership Conference (SCLC) had worked for years on voter registration. Starting with a project in Mississippi in 1961 and spreading through Georgia and Alabama, SNCC organized to register a great deal of people to vote, yet most were turned away from registering. Over and over they tried, but most were unsuccessful, facing the same types of barriers that Parks had, such as unfair tests, poll taxes, and hostile registrars. But SNCC kept pushing.

Finally, in 1964, Congress passed the Civil Rights Act—but it hadn't removed the many barriers to voting that Black people regularly confronted. So civil rights activists pressed on. In February 1965, twenty-six-year-old voting rights activist Jimmie Lee

Jackson was killed by police at a peaceful voting rights march in Marion, Alabama.

Activists with both SCLC and SNCC stepped up their work. To protest Jackson's death and the continued attacks on voting rights activists, SCLC organized a march from Selma to Alabama's state capitol in Montgomery. The protestors, led by John Lewis and the Reverend Hosea Williams, set out on March 7, 1965, and endured brutal attacks by police and state troopers on horseback wielding clubs on the Edmund Pettus Bridge, leading out of Selma. The violence was so bad it ended the march. The beatings were captured by television cameras, and the horrific images were broadcast nationally.

Dr. King and the SCLC refused to be stopped by the violence and instead decided to hold another march, putting out a call for people across the country to come to Selma. Moved by the photos of activists being beaten on the Edmund Pettus Bridge, Parks decided to return to her home state of Alabama to join the march herself. She couldn't afford the trip, but with help from her friend Louise Tappes, the United Auto Workers paid her way.

As the march entered its final stretch into Montgomery, Parks joined the last four-mile leg. The air reeked of stink bombs. And members of the White Citizens' Council had plastered the roads with huge billboards of a 1957 picture of Parks and Dr. King at Highlander Folk School, calling them Communists. The billboards felt ominous. A number of white people lined the march route and heckled her, sneering, "You'll get yours, Rosa."

Mrs. Parks had not been provided with a vest flagging her as an official participant, and so, without an official jacket, the police kept pulling her out of the

The Ku Klux Klan put up billboards painting Martin Luther King Jr. and Rosa Parks as Communists. Parks is on the far left.

march and making her stand on the sidelines. Many of the young people in attendance didn't know her, and so they didn't intervene. "I was in but they put me out," she said. "It seemed like such a short time that I had been out of Alabama, but so many young people had grown up in that time. They didn't know who I was." Away from the marchers, she got shoved repeatedly on the sidewalk.

A marshal recognized her and got her back in. She marched for a bit with Lillian Gregory, the wife of co-median Dick Gregory, as well as the blues-folk singer Odetta, whose music she loved. But Parks always ended up put back on the sidelines by the police, waiting for someone else to spot her and pull her back in. She would always think of being "put out of the march" when she looked back on the protest.

Speaking at the end of the Selma to Montgomery March

Upon its conclusion, a huge crowd gathered on the hill next to Montgomery's capitol building. Parks, along with Dr. King and a number of other leaders, gave speeches, which the news networks broadcast nationally. Introduced as the "first lady of the movement," Parks was coaxed to the podium by thunderous applause from the crowd. According to the *New Yorker* magazine, she received the most enthusiastic reception of all the speakers. In her remarks, she spoke about her personal history growing up under racism and her fear of KKK attacks. And instead of being frightened of the billboards posted along the march, she affirmed her connection to Highlander Folk School, highlighting what she had learned there and trying to counter "the propaganda" circulating about the school's Communist ties.

Mrs. Parks enjoyed seeing old friends at the march but felt Dr. King seemed "unusually shy" and "distracted." She got back to her hotel feeling tired and depressed. That night, she had a horrible nightmare. She dreamed she was standing in a huge field under a large billboard and saw a man with a gun; she was trying to warn Raymond when she realized the man with the gun aimed at her. Rosa woke up terrified.

Another Detroit resident who traveled to Alabama for the march was a white mother of five named Viola Liuzzo. Like Parks, she'd been moved by the photographs of the marchers being attacked on the Edmund Pettus Bridge and wanted to play her part. But as she shuttled marchers home and to the airport after the march, Liuzzo was murdered. Members of the KKK, including an FBI informant named Gary Rowe, pulled up alongside Liuzzo's car. They tried to force her off the road and shot at her and the other passenger, a nineteen-year-old Black man named Leroy Moton. But Moton outsmarted the terrorists; he pretended to be dead as the Klan members searched the car, and his life was spared.

Sickened by Liuzzo's death, Parks attended her memorial service back in Detroit. She also took part in a mass meeting the night before, calling for further commitment to the struggle. Liuzzo's murder spurred Parks to become even more politically active on a local level, particularly in the Women's Political Action Committee, which was headed by her friend Louise Tappes, and in the group Detroit Friends of SNCC.

Like other Friends of SNCC chapters, the Detroit branch fundraised for the work SNCC was doing in the South. Members educated Detroit residents of SNCC's ongoing efforts and also took up local issues. Rosa Parks and Dorothy Dewberry ran the local Friends chapter in the mid- to late 1960s. A Detroit native, Dewberry was a former NAACP youth chapter member and was a student at the Detroit Institute of Technology when she first met Parks.

Many Black people had migrated to Detroit from Alabama, just like the Parks family, and they still felt connected to what was happening in their old home and wanted to help support the movement. Through their experiences in the Selma march, a number of SNCC activists, including a young man named Stokely Carmichael, decided to try building an independent political movement in Lowndes County, Alabama. Lowndes County was located between Selma, where the march had started, and Montgomery, where it had ended.

SNCC had decided that they needed to build an independent Black political party because their allies in the Democratic Party didn't seem willing to ensure racial justice and real political access for Black people. The year before, after years of Black Mississippians being attacked and fired from their jobs for trying to register to vote, SNCC had created the Mississippi Freedom Democratic Party (MFDP) to highlight the discrimination promoted by the regular Mississippi Democratic Party. They hoped that all the evidence they brought and all the organizing they'd done would prompt the national Democratic Party to act. They wanted the Democratic Party either to refuse to seat the regular Mississippi Democratic delegation or to seat the MFDP (made up of sixty-four Black delegates, including civil rights leader Fannie Lou Hamer, and four white delegates) alongside the regular all-white Mississippi delegation at the 1964 Democratic National Convention.

The MFDP began receiving support from other state delegations. But, under pressure from President Lyndon Johnson who saw the MFDP as a threat, national Democratic leaders backed down when it came to ensuring Black voting rights and continued to seat the regular Mississippi Democratic delegation. Many allies who pledged support changed their minds and stopped pressing for the MFDP delegates to be seated. They said the problem would be fixed by the next convention . . . four years later. This led many in SNCC to feel they couldn't trust their supposed allies in the Democratic Party to stand firm for Black rights, and it launched SNCC's turn toward Black Power and its belief that Black people would need to build their own institutions and bases of power.

They would try it in Lowndes Country.

In 1965, not one Black person was registered to vote in this county, though many had tried. Meanwhile, the local politics were so corrupt that more white people were registered to vote than there were *actual white people in the county*. Most Lowndes residents, white and Black, were involved in agriculture. Preventing Black people from voting kept them living in poverty and at the mercy of white plantation owners and agricultural boards, which set the pricing of crops and goods. Building independent Black political power was a necessary step to ending this type of financial exploitation.

The Voting Rights Act was signed into law on August 6, 1965—the culmination of *two decades* of organizing. Rosa Parks attended the signing, seeing it as an incredible milestone for civil rights. But she knew this was just one step in the long road to securing racial justice. In a place like Lowndes County, the question was, How, if at all, would the new law be enforced?

Lowndes County was a violent place, particularly for people who challenged the way things had always been done, be they Black or white. In August 1965, white seminary student Jonathan Daniels had been protesting discriminatory treatment with other SNCC volunteers in

Fort Deposit, Alabama, and they were all arrested. Upon their release, he and three others, a white Catholic priest and two Black teenagers, walked into a store to buy a Coke and were assaulted by a white deputy named Tom Coleman. Coleman threatened the group and aimed his weapon at seventeen-year-old Ruby Sales. Jonathan Daniels reacted fast, jumping in front of her and pushing her down to protect her. He was killed instantly.

SNCC had researched Alabama law and realized it could create an independent political party. Stokely Carmichael moved to Lowndes County to begin building this party, which would be called the Lowndes County Freedom Organization.

Born in Trinidad, Carmichael, who later changed his name to Kwame Ture, had moved to Harlem when he was eleven years old and later attended Howard University. While there, he participated in the Freedom Rides and started working for SNCC full time in 1964.

Alabama had a law that allowed for the creation of new political parties; because many people in the state, both white and Black, could not read, any new party needed a symbol to identify it (so a person who couldn't read could still identify the party she or he wanted to vote for). The Lowndes County Freedom Organization chose a panther. As organizer John Hulett explained, the panther embodied their spirit: "The black panther is an animal that when it is pressured moves back until it is cornered, then it comes out fighting." The Alabama Democratic Party's symbol was a rooster—and these farmers knew from experience that cats hunted roosters—so the panther symbol displayed great power and strength. (The Black Panther Party for Self-Defense, which was founded in

Oakland, California, in 1966, got the idea to use the panther symbol from the Lowndes County movement.)

In March 1966, Rosa Parks and Dorothy Dewberry traveled to Alabama to support this independent Black political movement in Lowndes. They brought clothes and funds they'd raised from people in Detroit. Mrs. Parks spoke at their mass meeting celebrating the one-year anniversary of the Lowndes movement, praising their valiant organizing. On one of their trips, they were riding with Stokely Carmichael, a notoriously fast driver, on the dark and dangerous roads of Lowndes. Worried about an ambush, Dewberry began to panic, thinking, "We're going to kill the mother of the civil rights movement." She looked over at Parks, who appeared tranquil and unruffled. Mrs. Parks had been down similar roads before and had learned to manage her fear. Her serenity comforted Dewberry: "She had the effect of being able to calm people [by her composure]."

In October 1966, Carmichael, who'd been appointed chair of SNCC that May, came to Detroit to talk about Black Power. Thirteen hundred Black people and about fifty white people packed into Reverend Cleage's church to hear Carmichael speak. From the podium, he began by singling out Rosa Parks in the audience.

He called her his "hero."

# CHAPTER TWENTY-THREE

# THE DETROIT UPRISING

One of Rosa Parks's favorite spots in Detroit was a bookstore called Vaughn's. The owner, Ed Vaughn, worked at the post office and had begun selling books on Black culture, history, and literature from his car. There was such demand that he opened an official store in the early 1960s—the only Black bookstore in Detroit. Rosa and Raymond would stop by a couple of times a week to browse the books, as Rosa could never get enough Black history. Vaughn called her "one of my best customers."

Thursday evenings, the bookstore turned into a key meeting place for Detroit's Black activists—particularly the young radicals. Mrs. Parks attended regularly, along with the study circles that also met there. Being in community with other activists sustained her.

Frustration was mounting among Detroit's Black residents. Despite years of struggle, housing and schools had, if anything, grown *more* segregated. And while some jobs had opened up for Black

people in the city's auto industry, unemployment in the
community was still high.

Housing continued
to be an urgent problem.
White people—vigilantes
and police—often turned to
violence when Black people
moved into Detroit's all-white
suburbs or white sections of
the city. The majority of Black
people were crowded into
underserved neighborhoods
with escalating rents. The city
implemented urban renewal
efforts in some areas, claiming
they wanted to improve these
"slums." But, often, urban

Ed Vaughn and his bookstore

renewal meant that buildings and homes were torn down,
and, as a result, Black people lost their homes with no
better housing, business, or community opportunities.
Many of Parks's friends had nicknamed urban renewal
"Negro removal." Most times, the new housing options
that had been promised never materialized.

This increased tensions within the Black community.
Many of the activists who would become leaders in the
Black Power movement in the later 1960s spent the early
part of the decade highlighting the ravages of urban
renewal on Black Detroiters. The new Interstate High-
way System sliced right through Black neighborhoods,
isolating areas with many Black residents from the rest
of the city.

Despite many, many meetings, protests, and petitions, the civil rights movement in Detroit, as in many Northern cities, had produced little change in school segregation, housing segregation, or police misconduct in the city. White leaders and local citizens continued to do whatever they could to stop the movement from succeeding. Part of the difficulty was that most white residents thought the city offered great opportunity to Black people. They saw themselves as open and progressive, and many denied there was a problem, often blaming Black people for being too sensitive or lacking the right behaviors and values to succeed.

At the same time, Black migration to Northern cities wasn't slowing down—and considering the widespread segregation that was still in effect, Black neighborhoods grew increasingly crowded and underserved. So, over the 1960s, even as the civil rights movement heated up in the South, life for Black people in Detroit was getting worse.

Law enforcement enabled this pervasive inequality. The demographics of the police did not reflect Detroit's population. While the city was 35 percent Black, less than 5 percent of the police officers were; that meant that out of 4,709 officers, only 217 were African American, and only three of the 220 lieutenants were Black. On top of that, the police had a different relationship to Detroit's Black community, often treating Black Detroiters as a problem rather than seeing their mission to "protect and serve" Black as well as white residents.

Activists and groups like the NAACP had highlighted patterns of police brutality and harassment in the city for years, but Detroit's newspapers, city leaders, and many white residents chose to look the other way. According to Detroit NAACP leader Arthur Johnson, the local newspapers (the *Detroit News* and *Detroit Free Press*) had a standing agreement with the police to not cover incidents of police brutality. Only the Black newspapers reported these truths.

Bookstore owner Ed Vaughn described the police as "an army of occupation, [that would] ride down on us almost nightly." The officers were often disrespectful and regularly took money and other valuable items from the Black people they stopped. If Black people protested, this often led to a beating or a false charge of drunkenness, disorderly conduct, or resisting arrest.

The Detroit police had expanded the practice of arresting Black people simply on "investigation"; in fact, one-third of their arrestees were arrested without charge, just on investigation. The police also used new federal funds in 1965 to create a tactical mobile unit for "crowd control," which was abusive to Black people in many cases. At the meetings in Vaughn's bookstore, the Black community expressed frustration over this unjust treatment and police brutality. They were tired of having their concerns brushed aside by white politicians and fellow Detroit residents.

Things had reached a boiling point.

The Detroit Riot—which people like Rosa Parks called a "rebellion" or an "uprising"—started less than a mile from where the Parkses lived. On the evening of July 23, 1967, people had gathered at an illegal after-hours bar (known as a "blind pig") at 9125 Twelfth Street. They were celebrating the safe return home of two men from the war in Vietnam.

Many Black people socialized on Twelfth Street because of its numerous bars, clubs, and other Black businesses. When cops raided the blind pig at 4:00 a.m., patrons refused to disperse. This was a political act. Many Detroit entertainment venues and restaurants banned Black patrons, and Black business owners often had difficulty securing the permits for an official establishment, so working-class Black people often met up in these kinds of bars. And they were regularly raided by police—a chief source of frustration for Black Detroit residents before the uprising. The evening of July 23 was the third time this bar had been raided in less than two years.

The police began arresting people, and the crowd grew larger and angrier as morning dawned. And as the day went on, the police grew more violent and forceful. The unrest spread. Some people set fires or looted stores—especially businesses that had treated Black people poorly or overcharged them for items. At the peak of the unrest, the uprising spread out to fourteen square miles.

The governor requested federal help, and soon, 2,700 army paratroopers descended on the city. Tanks rolled through Detroit, and the mayor declared a curfew, which meant people out on the streets after 5:00 p.m. could be arrested. Law enforcement was allowed to "subdue" the uprising by any means necessary, so they arrested thousands of people and roughed up many in the process. At the end of the five days, forty-three people were dead—thirty at the hands of the police—and the city estimated property damage at $45 million, with 412 buildings completely burned to the ground.

Michigan congressman John Conyers later described Detroit's 1967 uprising as a "police riot." They made over 7,200 arrests, the majority of which were later found to be without reason. The police arrested so many people that they turned Belle Isle Park into a jail and started holding people in buses. The police shot out the street-lights and raided apartments where supposed rioters were hiding, arresting and assaulting many uninvolved citizens. Perhaps the worst incident took place at the Algiers Motel on the night of July 25, where police killed three Black teenagers: Carl Cooper, age seventeen; Aubrey Pollard, age nineteen; and Fred Temple, age eighteen. While police claimed a gunfight, no weapons were ever found, and witnesses said the young men were deliberately murdered.

Ed Vaughn's bookstore was firebombed by the police, who tried to blame the act on neighborhood thugs. Then the police and fire department broke into the store to put out the fire but left the water running, ruining nearly all the books inside. The police also shattered the pictures of Dr. King and Malcolm X that lined the wall.

Conyers's Detroit office, where Parks worked, became a hub of information and a complaint center during the uprising—with many people reporting police misconduct. Parks participated in many meetings trying to address community concerns with law enforcement.

Most judges refused to intervene against this police abuse. Wayne County prosecutor William Cahalan asked judges to set extremely high bails so people would stay locked up and "off the streets." And most judges went along with this, abandoning their responsibility to be a check on law enforcement practices and instead acting as if they worked for the prosecutor's office.

But newly elected Black judge George Crockett re-fused to set high bails. Most of the arrests the police had made didn't hold up, and a year later, the vast majority of the cases had been dismissed for lack of evidence. Only a small number actually resulted in the arrested person being convicted on the original charges. Judge Crockett was sickened by the way his fellow judges were swayed by the police and the mayor's office during the uprising.

Crockett grew up in Jacksonville, Florida, and then attended Morehouse College. After he graduated from the University of Michigan Law School, he served as a criminal defense lawyer and national vice president of the National Lawyers Guild. He was part of the legal team in 1949 that defended eleven Communist leaders who were accused of wanting to overthrow the government because of their beliefs in Communism. Crockett himself was thrown in jail for four months because the judge didn't like how strongly Crockett was defending his clients.

In 1966, he decided to run for Detroit's Recorder's Court so he could become a judge and do things differently. He observed that "there is no equal justice for Black people in our criminal courts today, and what's more, there never has been. And this is the shame of our whole judicial system. . . . And this is so, not because the written law says it shall be so, rather it is so because our judges, by their rulings, make it so."

Crockett ultimately used his powers as a judge to try to right the scales; he often gave first-time offenders and nonviolent offenders lenient sentences and set low or no bails. He refused to approve police tactics without questioning their value or to simply follow along with prosecutors on how things should proceed. During the uprising, he refused the prosecutor's wishes to set high bail, and he let those arrested have access to attorneys.

■   ■   ■

Raymond Parks grew increasingly upset during the uprising. He went out into the fray to try to protect the barbershop, but the shop was looted and some of his equipment was stolen. His and Rosa's new car was also vandalized. He was accosted by a police officer who "threatened to hit him on the head with a rifle" and took a small knife Raymond was carrying, a treasured gift from a client back in Montgomery. The stress of the events caused another nervous breakdown, and Rosa had to drive Raymond to get a sedative so he could calm down.

Rosa Parks was greatly saddened by the destruction of the uprising. She didn't think it "was going to accomplish any good," but she still saw the rebellion as "the result of resistance to change that was needed long beforehand." Indeed, in a survey of Black Detroiters after the uprising, 82 percent said that police brutality was a key problem leading to the rebellion.

Parks believed you had to look at the long history of white resistance to Black equality to understand where the uprising had come from: "The [political] establishment of white people . . . will antagonize and provoke violence. When the young people want to present themselves as human beings and come into their own as men, there is always something to cut them down." She felt that if Black people had been treated more equally, and if their demands for housing desegregation, school equity, better city services, more well-paying jobs, and proper treatment from police had been met, there never would have been an uprising.

Ed Vaughn echoed this sentiment. Black Detroit residents had been protesting Detroit's racism for years, but the city refused to budge. As he said, "Everybody who cares, white and Black, told them. They did not listen."

A few months later, in a talk for the American Psychological Association, Dr. King reframed the question of riots by highlighting the actions and crimes of white people that had led to them: "When we ask Negroes to abide by the law, let us also demand that the white man abide by law in the ghettos. Day in and day out, he violates welfare laws to deprive the poor of their meager allotments; he flagrantly violates building codes and regulations; his police make a mockery of law; and he violates laws on equal employment and education and the provisions for civic services."

Following the uprising, Rosa Parks took up two initiatives to help the community move forward. First was the need to address police brutality. The city had decided not to charge the officers in killing the three young men at the Algiers Motel. On top of that injustice, the media refused to press the issue. So the real story of what happened to these three teenagers was being buried.

Tired of the lack of accountability, Black Power activists decided to hold a People's Tribunal on the police killings as a form of community justice. This meant they would hold their own trial to expose the full story of what happened that night. On the suggestion of SNCC chair H. Rap Brown, young radicals, led by Dan Aldridge and Lonnie Peek, organized the tribunal as a way "to bring out all the facts and truth about what actually happened" at the Algiers Motel. Aldridge, who had married Parks's friend Dorothy Dewberry, was aware of Rosa Parks's community stature and broad politics, so he asked if she would serve on the jury. She said if her presence would be helpful, she was happy to do so. This was an act of inner strength on her part; Parks knew the family of Carl Cooper (one of the teenagers who'd been killed), and the uprising had been hard on Rosa's own family. But she set aside her personal pain to take part.

The People's Tribunal took place in Reverend Cleage's church, announced by a flyer that said: "Review and watch the evidence for yourself."

More than two thousand Black people and a smattering of white people crammed into the church on the evening of August 30, 1967. The trial was held in the sanctuary under an eighteen-foot image of the Black Madonna, painted by Detroit artist Glanton Dowdell. Reverend Cleage had installed the painting at the front of the church earlier that year so "we can conceive of the Son of God being born of a Black woman." (After that, the church came to be known as the Shrine of the Black Madonna.)

Thousands of people packed Rev. Cleage's church for the People's Tribunal.

Those gathered that night heard the case against three white Detroit police officers: Ronald August, Robert Paille, and David Sendak, as well as a Black security guard named Melvin Dismukes. The witnesses vividly recounted the evening's events. The four were charged in what witnesses described as the "execution" of Carl Cooper, Aubrey Pollard, and Fred Temple at the Manor House annex of the Algiers Motel. Witnesses were kept out of sight until the final minute for fear of police intimidation and retaliation. (The Detroit Bar Association considered disbarring the lawyers who participated in the trubunal.)

Twelve people served on the jury, including Parks, Black novelist John O. Killens, Black bookstore owner Ed Vaughn, and two white people, Patricia Murphy and Frank Joyce. Journalists from as far away as France and Sweden covered the event. The jury found the officers guilty of murder. According to Aldridge, the reaction following the convictions was "joy. . . . Because they heard the truth."

Along with trying to address police brutality, Parks joined a community development effort to get a shopping center at the location where the uprising had started. Black Detroit neighborhoods didn't have enough grocery stores—and Parks was a firm believer in locally grown food and the need for fresh fruits and vegetables. So she helped form the Virginia Park District Council.

Many years later, in 1981, the council finally broke ground on one of the only community-owned Black shopping developments in the *nation*.

And Rosa Parks was one of its best customers.

# CHAPTER TWENTY-FOUR

# THE ASSASSINATION OF DR. KING

When Rosa Parks traveled to the wealthy and segregated Detroit suburb of Grosse Pointe to see Dr. Martin Luther King speak, she didn't know it would be the last time she'd see him.

It was March 14, 1968, fourteen years after they'd first met in Montgomery. Parks and a friend were looking forward to seeing King speak at Grosse Pointe High School. Instead, they found a "mess." White residents "disrupted the meeting," Parks said. "It was an all-white city."

And they relentlessly heckled Dr. King. The high school had been forced to take out extra insurance when they decided to host him—and the police were so worried about threats on Dr. King's life that the local police chief sat on King's lap to protect him as they drove him up to the building. King described it as the most disruptive indoor crowd he'd ever encountered.

That evening, Dr. King called out the pervasive racism of Detroit and its suburbs. Like Parks, he insisted that Northerners address the problems in their own backyards instead of just pointing fingers at the South. While many white Detroiters used the uprising of the previous summer as evidence that Black people were of poor character, Dr. King insisted that they see the uprising's larger context:

> It is not enough for me to stand before you tonight and condemn riots. It would be morally irresponsible for me to do that without, at the same time, condemning the contingent, intolerable conditions that exist in our society. . . . A riot is the language of the unheard. And what is it that America has failed to hear? It has failed to hear that the plight of the Negro poor has worsened over the last twelve or fifteen years. It has failed to hear that the promises of freedom and justice have not been met. And it has failed to hear that large segments of white society are more concerned about tranquility and the status quo than about justice and humanity.

Throughout the 1960s, King repeatedly criticized Northerners' shallow commitment to civil rights. While many Northerners supported change in the South, when it came to their hometowns, they refused to see the problems in front of them. Referring to the suburbs as "white nooses around the Black necks of the cities," King also observed how "housing deteriorates in central cities" while "suburbs expand with little regard for what happens to the rest of America."

Unlike some of their Southern counterparts who defended segregation explicitly, Northern whites found different explanations to excuse their segregated schools and housing and abusive policing. They faulted Black culture and community values for crime, poverty, and inequalities in housing and schools. King critiqued this, laying the responsibility on the "white majority . . . [for] producing chaos" while blaming the chaos on Black people and claiming that if they behaved better, success would come their way. Focusing on Black crime, he said, was a way to avoid looking at the much greater crime of ghettoizing people in communities with insufficient schools, jobs, and city services. "It is incontestable and deplorable that Negroes have committed crimes; but they are derivative crimes . . . born of the greater crimes of the white society."

For Reverend King, the ways white people ignored injustice around them—or claimed to have nothing to do with it—was a sin. He reminded audiences across the nation that the "summers of riots" were caused by the "winters of delay."

That evening in Grosse Pointe, many people in the audience yelled nasty comments at Dr. King. They interrupted him repeatedly, calling him a traitor. They resented him and what he had to say. They preferred that King focus on the South and didn't like it when he turned the spotlight on their own cities, actions, and inactions. At one point King responded to the hecklers, saying there would be a Q&A session where they could discuss his "traitorness." This was not unusual for King; after all, he'd been met with tremendous hostility all over the country—in Chicago, Birmingham, Los Angeles, Detroit, Atlanta, and beyond.

Many white people across the country saw King as anti-American, and they weren't afraid to tell him so. Today, King is widely honored, but back in 1966, nearly three-quarters of Americans disapproved of him and his work. Many picketed his appearances, calling him un-American and an extremist. They criticized his tactics for being too disruptive. This was a national phenomenon. In 1966, King said he had "never seen—even in Mississippi and Alabama—mobs as hostile and as hate-filled as I've seen here in Chicago." And that night in Grosse Pointe, Michigan, was one of the most disturbing displays of opposition he'd ever seen. Because the scene was so disorderly, Mrs. Parks didn't even get to talk to him.

Just three weeks after seeing him speak, Rosa was listening to the radio with her mother when the broadcast was interrupted with an announcement:

> DR. MARTIN LUTHER KING JR. WAS SHOT WHILE
> LEAVING HIS MOTEL ROOM IN MEMPHIS.

Devastated, Parks began crying over the news of her friend. Calls started coming into her house about the shooting. "He can't die, I said to myself, he can't die," she thought.

An hour later, at 7:05 p.m., Dr. King was pronounced dead. "I went numb," Parks said. That evening, she found solace in Sam Cooke's song "A Change Is Gonna Come," playing it over and over. The song was soothing; it almost felt like Dr. King was talking to her.

Her friend Louise Tappes called, and they decided to head to Memphis to support the sanitation workers' strike King had been assisting before he was killed. Raymond thought it was a bad idea for her to go. But, still in tears, she decided it was important to go. In Memphis, she talked with the striking workers but after a few hours was overcome with grief and had to leave. She accepted singer Harry Belafonte's invitation to fly on his plane to Atlanta for King's funeral.

The assassination settled over Parks like a heavy blanket. Just as she'd felt in the years before the boycott, "it was hard to keep going when our efforts seemed in vain." But, never one to let herself stop even when she felt dejected, Parks took up the work of the Poor People's Campaign (PPC), a multiracial movement King was helping to build when he was assassinated and which his widow, Coretta Scott King, and poor people from across the country carried forward.

The idea for the campaign had originated from a 1966 visit Dr. King made to a Head Start day-care center in Marks, Mississippi. Four children had sat there, eagerly awaiting a lunch that consisted of nothing more than a quarter of an apple. And King, normally composed, had broken down into tears. "I can't get those children out of my mind," he later told SCLC activist Ralph Abernathy, who'd visited the poor, sharecropping community with him. "I don't think people really know that little school-children are slowly starving in the United States of America."

Part of the Poor People's Campaign's aim was to force the country to "see the

THE ASSASSINATION OF DR. KING ■ 237

poor" and compel Congress to act. The plan was that poor people of all races and ethnicities—African American, Latinx, Native American, Asian American, and white—from all across the country would descend on Washington, DC, to demand "$30 billion annual appropriation for a real war on poverty; Congressional passage of full employment and guaranteed income legislation [a guaranteed annual wage]; and Construction of 500,000 low-cost housing units per year." The PPC linked the struggle for racial justice to economic justice and the need for a real safety net for poor families, denouncing the ways that people receiving welfare or food assistance were often shamed. They saw how poor people of different races were taught to see each other as the problem—and so they worked to overcome that and build a broadly multiracial movement.

On May 12, 1968, PPC organizers broke ground in Washington, DC, setting up a tent city of plywood shanties on the National Mall that they named Resurrection City. Nine caravans of poor people of all races and ethnicities began making their way across the country to DC. The most visible Black caravan with one hundred people and seventeen mule-drawn wagons started out from Marks, Mississippi, the poorest county in the country. Coretta Scott King launched a caravan from Memphis, the site of King's assassination. And caravans of Native American and Latinx people traveled thousands of miles from California and the Southwest.

The high point of the campaign was June 19, Solidarity Day. Rosa Parks journeyed to Washington to take part. More than fifty thousand people gathered to hear Coretta Scott King, Parks, and others speak about the

need to fight racism, poverty, and war. Introduced to
a thunderous ovation, Mrs.
Parks choked up, saying she
was so glad to be there but
how she wished Reverend
King could be there with
them too.

The PPC challenged the
idea that people caused their
own poverty, highlighting the
policies that kept people poor.
The speakers demanded programs for full employment,
a guaranteed annual income,
and the construction of more
affordable housing. Coretta

Speaking at Solidarity Day
of the Poor People's Campaign

Scott King also criticized the hypocrisy of the United
States promoting itself as a land of opportunity when
poor Americans were hurt and oppressed. She reminded
the nation: "Neglecting school children is violence. Pun-
ishing a mother and her family is violence. . . . Ignoring
medical needs is violence. Contempt for poverty is violence. Even the lack of will power to help humanity is a
sick and sinister form of violence."

Although its demands were clear, the Poor People's
Campaign was criticized by many in Congress and the
media as "unruly" and needing "clarity." Many news
organizations ran unflattering stories or cast the PPC as
the problem. Many in the government didn't want the
PPC in town. The FBI had massively monitored the caravans and many of the PPC organizers—and the Pentagon

had twenty thousand troops on standby as soon as the campaign had arrived in DC. Resurrection City was torn down by the police on June 24, 1968.

Parks was demoralized by King's assassination, as were many activists across the country—even those who hadn't agreed with King's emphasis on nonviolence.

Shortly after the murder of King, Parks told a reporter that she was unsure she could be "as strong, forgiving, and Christian-like as Dr. King. Sometimes I think it's asking too much, in the face of all the oppression and abuse we have to bear."

# CHAPTER TWENTY-FIVE

# BLACK POWER!

Like many younger activists, Rosa Parks had grown frustrated with the extent of white opposition to civil rights.

To Parks, ongoing white resistance to change had planted the seeds for more militant Black politics to grow. Parks was a kind woman, raised in the church and the Southern traditions of maintaining good manners and a good public face. She displayed a reserved demeanor and a wealth of patience and self-control.

But that didn't mean she wasn't furious at the depth and breadth of American racism. Time and again, she tried to show the roots and legitimacy of Black rebellion. She was livid that Black people were often told to wait for justice to come—to be patient and not to get angry. Parks had long hated the ways Black rebels were seen as freaks or demonized for their refusal to submit to white supremacy.

Many Americans—and politicians across the country—criticized Black Power. In a 1970 interview, Parks tried to put the growing Black Power movement in context. She reminded the interviewer about the ways many white people had attacked King's nonviolent movement:

> Dr. King was criticized because he tried to bring about change through the nonviolent movement. It didn't accomplish what it should have because the white Establishment would not accept his philosophy of nonviolence and respond to it positively. When the resistance grew, it created a hostility and bitterness among the younger people, who worked with him in the early days, when there was some hope that change could be accomplished through his means.

Rosa Parks didn't stop fighting after Dr. King's assassination.

To her, the criticisms of Black Power, like those leveled at King, had a key similarity: many Americans treated those who pushed hard against racial injustice as the problem and refused to change. This laid the groundwork for Black Power.

According to Black Power activist Dan Aldridge, people were often surprised by how consistently Parks attended Black Power events; she was so ladylike and genteel, but there was depth to her politics and an unwillingness to back down. "Quiet and sweet but strong as acid," bookstore owner

Ed Vaughn characterized her. He remembered Parks as being everywhere in the late 1960s and 1970s: "Honest to God, almost every meeting I went to, she was always there." When a reporter asked in 1974 how she managed to do so much, she simply said, "I do what I can."

About eight months after the uprising, the Parks family bought a car from her brother Sylvester, a huge, white Ford sedan. And it was quite a sight to behold the small Rosa Parks driving herself around town in that big white car to attend Black Power meetings, lectures, and rallies.

The most prevalent image of Black Power is of a Black man wearing a black leather jacket and beret, carrying a gun, with a fist in the air. But Black Power activists were a diverse group. They didn't all dress a certain way or talk a certain way. Many, many women organized and led during the Black Power movement. While Black Power activists were often portrayed as hard, a love of humanity ran through many people's activism. That love made Mrs. Parks and many of her Black Power associates tender toward people's suffering and inpatient with the lack of change. They could not rest easy in the face of continuing injustice.

Rosa Parks was a shy, middle-aged woman who often dressed conservatively *and* supported a variety of Black Power ideas and initiatives. Many of the goals of Black Power were ones that she'd been fighting to achieve for a long time. As Congressman John Conyers said, Parks was a "progressive but she did not wear her political philosophy on her sleeve."

Parks also lent support to the actions young Black Power activists were taking. She didn't feel as if she had to lead or tell this younger generation how to do things.

"If I can be helpful, I will come" was her message to young militants asking her to take part in various actions, like the People's Tribunal. And show up she did, over and over. "Dang, it's Rosa again," Vaughn thought as he spotted her all over the city. Unity and collective support for the actions that others were organizing was key to Parks's philosophy.

In many ways, her political approach resembled her quilting skills. "Any good woman my age from Alabama definitely knows how to quilt," she said. Her respect for ancestry and appreciation for conserving a Black past—sewing many pieces together and bringing together several different materials—resonated with strands of Black Power in this period.

Black Power did not ruin the quilt of Black protest for Rosa Parks—it enriched it. And Black Power drew on pieces already there. Above all, the need for people to work together and resist division, for people to pitch in to assist the actions of others, was a core part of her beliefs: "In quilting, maybe somebody would come in to visit, it might be a friend, and would just join in and help," she said. She believed in a united front approach—that it would take many tactics and approaches to win justice and freedom—so she supported a whole variety of groups and actions.

Parks "spoke with her presence," Conyers explained. In late August 1968, she attended the Black Power Convention in Philadelphia. There, as she did at many Black Power events, she sat near the front, often with Queen Mother Moore, sewing or doing other handwork to keep herself busy while she listened. A young militant named Max Stanford of the Revolutionary Action Movement remembered how delighted and surprised he was when a friend, the Black scholar and psychologist Nathan Hare, introduced him to Mrs. Parks. There she was, just soaking in the convention.

Like many Black Power activists, both Queen Mother Moore and Rosa Parks believed that Black people were owed reparations from the government for the injustices of slavery and segregation. Black people's labor, skill, and taxes had been taken and used for centuries to build wealth, including home ownership, for other Americans and for the country at large. Therefore, they were owed compensation for this stolen labor, talent, and wealth. In 1994, the National Coalition of Blacks for Reparations in America held its first meeting. Sitting in the front row were Queen Mother Moore and Rosa Parks.

They were also critical of US foreign policy. Parks had been passionately opposed to the United States' involvement in the Vietnam War since the early 1960s, and she had spoken out against it even when it was dangerous to do so. Part of why she'd supported John Conyers in 1964 was because he, too, was an early opponent of the country's intervention in Vietnam. Watching as the war drained resources that could address poverty and social issues at home, she also saw that the war was motivated by a vicious anti-Communist stance that had little to do with the needs and desires of the Vietnamese people—the majority of whom would have supported the Communist Ho Chi Minh if the United States hadn't blocked their elections. Black men were dying in high numbers in combat in Southeast Asia when they were denied equal justice and nondiscriminatory treatment at home.

As part of her work in Conyers office, Parks met with veterans' groups and returning soldiers. Men returning from Vietnam made up a significant wing of the antiwar movement, and many of these veterans formed Vietnam Veterans Against the War (VVAW). Mrs. Parks was a strong supporter, including of the Winter Soldier hearings VVAW organized in 1971 to publicize the atrocities occurring in Vietnam. She also attended numerous meetings, rallies, and teach-ins on the war at Wayne State University. She'd long been part of the Women's International League for Peace and Freedom, and she was listed with Coretta Scott King as one of the sponsors of the women-led Jeannette Rankin Brigade antiwar protest, held in Washington, DC, on January 15, 1968.

Seeing Rosa Parks at so many Black Power events meant a lot to younger activists. Encouraged to have her on their side, they felt protected and that they were standing on the shoulders of other Black freedom fighters. This solidarity across generations was precious—particularly because Parks trusted young people to find their way and was not the type of activist to tell others how to do things. Black Panther Party activist Ericka Huggins emphasized the tremendous regard she and other Panthers held for Rosa Parks, saying how incredible it was when Parks decided to visit the Black Panther Party school.

The Black Panther Party started many community programs as part of its serve-the-people focus, including free breakfast programs, free medical clinics, and an independent elementary school in Oakland, California. The Panthers started the school to address the ways Black children were being undereducated in Oakland's schools; the children were punished too often and not provided with the literacy and math skills needed, nor the proper background in Black history and culture.

Visiting the Black Panther school. Director Ericka Huggins is at the right.

Parks was delighted to visit the school in 1980, where students performed a play they'd written in her honor. She was so excited about what they were doing at the school, she stayed there for hours. Ericka Huggins ran the school, and she and the other staff were extremely touched by Mrs. Parks's visit. They talked about it for weeks.

Rosa Parks was moved by the cultural politics of the time, as well. She began wearing dashikis and other clothing made from or inspired by African fabrics and styles. She loved attending the many lectures on Black history and culture that bloomed around the city of Detroit. The importance of Black history—and the need to add it to every school curriculum—had long been deeply important to Parks. Since she was a little girl, she'd recognized Black history as a key weapon in the fight against white supremacy. During the era of Black Power, learning opportunities exploded.

Parks had been a huge reader since childhood, and as an adult, she followed a number of newspapers and magazines each day, diligently reading local, national, and international news. She subscribed to various Black newspapers, including the *Birmingham World* and the *Michigan Chronicle*, as well as militant publications, from the Southern Conference Educational Fund's *Southern Patriot* and *Now!*, the paper of the Freedom Now Party, to the *Detroit Community Voice* and Wayne State's student newspaper, the *South End*. She often saved issues of these papers to reread and clipped hundreds of articles on Black history and the Black Power movement, passing them around to friends. Friends remembered the Parkses' home was piled high with books, newspapers, and magazines.

Another key aspect of Black Power was building the political power of Black people. This meant ensuring that candidates of any race took on the issues important to the Black community and electing more Black people to office. Independent Black politics was not a new concept to Rosa Parks. Back in 1950s Montgomery with E. D. Nixon, she'd been convinced of the power of an organized Black vote. In the early 1960s, Mrs. Parks had supported the Freedom Now Party, a Black political party her friends the Reverend Cleage and brothers Milton and Richard Henry were trying to start in Michigan. And she'd gone to Lowndes County in 1966 to support the independent Black party SNCC was building there.

Just as she had done with Conyers's run for Congress, Parks was committed to getting more Black people elected to public office. She volunteered on many local campaigns, willing to do the nitty-gritty office work—from George Crockett's campaign for recorder's court judge in 1966 to Coleman Young's successful bid to become Detroit's first Black mayor, in 1973.

In 1968, Parks was part of a group of Black delegates who refused to endorse any presidential candidate at the Democratic National Convention in Chicago, seeing none of them as sufficiently committed to prioritizing Black community issues or encouraging Black leadership.

The National Black Political Convention grew from this stance. It was held in Gary, Indiana, March 10–12, 1972. A presidential election was going to take place that year, and the convention brought ten thousand Black people from across the country to outline an independent Black political agenda. Many had grown tired of the empty promises from Democratic *and* Republican leaders. Organized Black Power would make both parties take Black issues more seriously. Parks served on the staff of the Gary convention and offered a brief greeting at the opening, giving her blessings for the event.

Unfortunately, despite the vital issues that were discussed, the convention refused to support the one Black person running for president that year: New York congresswoman Shirley Chisholm. Announcing her candidacy on January 25, 1972, Chisholm said:

> I stand before you today as a candidate for the Democratic nomination for the presidency of the United States of America. I am not the candidate of Black America, although I am Black and proud. I am not the candidate of the women's movement of this country, although I am a woman and I'm equally proud of that. . . . Those of you who were locked outside of the convention hall in 1968, those of you who can now

vote for the first time, those of you who agree with me that the institutions of this country belong to all of the people who inhabit it, those of you who have been neglected, left out, ignored, forgotten, or shunned aside for whatever reason, give me your help at this hour.

Chisholm had been elected as the first Black congresswoman in 1968 from a newly drawn district in Brooklyn. Having grown up in Brooklyn and Barbados, Chisholm attended Brooklyn College, taught in a nursery school, and then became active in Democratic politics. She was elected to the state assembly in 1965, then went on to defeat CORE leader James Farmer while running on an "unbought and unbossed" platform for the Twelfth Congressional District of New York.

On June 28, 1969, Chisholm made her first public appearance in Detroit. Parks gave the introduction, describing the congresswoman as a "pepper pot." She highlighted Chisholm's family roots in the Marcus Garvey movement—like her own—and celebrated Chisholm's "defiance and loyalty to her constituents." Parks also spotlighted the role Chisholm's husband, Conrad, played as "her closest friend and advisor," as Raymond was for Rosa.

When Shirley Chisholm decided to run for president, Parks supported her bid for the Democratic nomination. However, many of the leaders of the Gary Convention were men who felt that a Black man was better suited for the position.

Rosa Parks and Shirley Chisholm

So they didn't endorse her campaign. Though groups like the Black Panther Party supported Chisholm, she didn't secure the nomination. Instead, George McGovern was named the Democratic candidate—and Parks worked determinedly for him as well.

Another aim of Black Power was to confront the injustices embedded in the criminal justice system. In the 1960s and 1970s, this increasingly meant taking on the cases of Black political prisoners. State prosecutors brought charges against many activists, often falsifying charges as a way to discredit them and stop their work. Former NAACP leader Robert Williams was one person targeted by these tactics.

Parks had long admired Williams for his leadership of the NAACP chapter in Monroe, North Carolina. Like Parks and Nixon had done in Montgomery, Williams and his wife, Mabel, rebuilt their local NAACP chapter in the late 1950s into a more activist, working-class chapter. But the national NAACP office was displeased when Williams told Black people to arm themselves, stating that ongoing white violence had made Black self-defense necessary. As a result, the NAACP suspended him.

Williams also believed in the power of organized nonviolence, participating in sit-ins in Monroe, all the while affirming the right to self-defense alongside them. Then, in 1961, during racial unrest in Monroe following the Freedom Rides, Robert Williams sheltered a white couple in his home after they'd mistakenly ended up in the Black community. The FBI accused him of kidnapping and put out a warrant for Williams. He and his family escaped, first traveling to Cuba, where he published a book, *Negroes with Guns*, and ran a radio show, *Radio*

*Free Dixie*, and then to China. After eight years in exile, the Williams family was allowed to return to the United States. They settled in Detroit, where Robert still had to fight his extradition to North Carolina to face charges of kidnapping. Parks helped raise attention and funds for his case. In turn, Williams was alarmed that people didn't seem to understand Rosa Parks's crucial contributions to the struggle, and his wife, Mabel, recalled how he spoke about her at public events around his case. North Carolina dropped the charges against Williams in 1975.

Back in Detroit at Conyers's office, Rosa Parks used her position to try to advocate for better and more humane treatment for prisoners. She was active on a number of political-prisoner cases, including those for the Wilmington 10, Joan Little, and Angela Davis. When Angela Davis was freed and traveled to Detroit for a rally, Parks was the one to introduce her.

Parks helped found the Detroit chapter of the Free Joan Little campaign. Little had been in jail for burglary when her jailer, Clarence Alligood, threatened her with an ice pick and forced her to perform oral sex. Little managed to grab the ice pick, stabbed Alligood, and escaped, turning herself in to police days later.

Beginning with Recy Taylor's and Gertrude Perkins's cases decades earlier, Parks had long fought for a woman's right to be free from violence and sexual coercion. Ever since she sat out on the front porch with her shotgun-bearing grandfather, she believed people had the right to defend themselves from violence, even women in jail. Parks was one of the people put in charge of soliciting help from other organizations. Free Joan Little campaigns grew in many cities around the country. In part because of these efforts, Joan Little was eventually acquitted.

Many prisoners wrote to Rosa Parks in her position at Conyers's office, and she did what she could for them. Radical lawyer Chokwe Lumumba recounted how Parks intervened to ensure the safety of Republic of New Afrika (RNA) members after they were arrested. Founded in 1968 by activists in Detroit including Parks's friends Richard and Milton Henry (who now took the names Imari and Gaidi Obadele), the Republic of New Afrika was built on the principles that the government owed Black people reparations in the form of land. They advocated for the five states of the Deep South becoming an independent Black-majority nation.

In 1970, a group of RNA members secured a farm and moved to Jackson, Mississippi, to begin the process of acquiring more land for Black people. Law enforcement didn't like this, and the FBI began heavily monitoring the organization. In August 1971, the FBI and Jackson police raided the RNA farm with guns, tear gas, and a tank. A shootout between the police and RNA members ensued; one Jackson police officer was killed, and another officer and FBI agent were wounded. Eleven RNA members, including the president, Imari Obadele—who was not even on the farm that day—were arrested. The police began brutalizing the suspects, including a pregnant woman, marching them half-naked through the streets.

A neighbor phoned RNA minister of justice Chokwe Lumumba back in Detroit and told him what was happening. Frantic that the RNA members would be killed in police custody, Lumumba called Congressman Conyers's office to ask for help and intervention. Rosa Parks was the one who got on the phone that day, and she began calling and calling until the Department of Justice assured her the suspects would be treated humanely. Lumumba believed she saved their lives that day.

After the RNA members were convicted, Parks continued phoning the prison, making clear that it was "Rosa Parks from Congressman Conyers's office" calling, so officials knew they were being watched. Conyers said later that Obadele "often told me that the actions of Rosa Parks saved his life in that Mississippi jail."

Rosa Parks was doing so much political work and traveling so often that she asked her brother, Sylvester, if her niece Rhea could move in to help care for Raymond and their mother, Leona, when she was away. Sylvester said yes, and Rhea joined the Parks family in their Virginia Park flat. This arrangement ended after a year because Leona only wanted Rosa taking care of her. For many years, Raymond's public activism had lessened, but he still championed Rosa's behind the scenes, helping her make travel arrangements and supporting her busy schedule.

For many activists like Parks, the late 1960s and 1970s were a time of both new possibilities and growing frustration. While she was heartened by the younger generation of Black Power activists and all they were doing, the enormity of white resistance to change and government repression weighed on her. Throughout the 1950s, 1960s, and 1970s, those who challenged the racial status quo were often called extremists and investigated by the local police and the FBI. In fact, the FBI's spying on Dr. King had *expanded* after the March on Washington to include his home, office, hotel rooms—every place he went. The surveillance got even worse after King denounced US policy in Vietnam in 1967 . . . and continued up until his assassination, in 1968.

He wasn't the only person the FBI monitored, though; from Coretta Scott King to Ella Baker to SNCC to the Black Panther Party, the organization had eyes on many other civil rights activists. The FBI's treatment of Black activists perpetuated two major societal harms.

First, the FBI's surveillance and monitoring disrupted the movement, particularly through its COINTELPRO (an abbreviation of Counterintelligence Program) efforts in the late 1960s and 1970s. In 1967, the FBI reformulated its COINTELPRO program, which had begun in 1956 to attack Communist organizations. Now it would "disrupt, misdirect, discredit, or otherwise neutralize the activities of Black nationalist hate type organizations." In other words, the FBI sought to stop or discredit the activities of many Black Power groups, which at times led to violence.

The next year, with COINTELPRO and Project Z, a program to "prevent the rise of a Black Messiah" (the FBI specifically named King, Stokely Carmichael, and Elijah Muhammad as dangerous), the FBI took special measures to combat Black leaders they regarded as too powerful. They wanted to prevent the growth of the Black Power movement, particularly among young people. In the first years of COINTELPRO, the FBI particularly targeted the Black Panther Party. The agency worked with Chicago police in a 1969 raid that killed Black Panther leaders Fred Hampton and Mark Clark, and it spread misinformation to spark rivalries and violent revenge between Black groups. As the bureau sent an army of Black informants into groups like the Black Panther Party, it finally desegregated its own ranks and developed a large unit of Black people who spied on various Black groups and political leaders. (FBI director J. Edgar Hoover had resisted hiring Black people, except to do menial jobs, until 1962.) By the 1970s, the FBI also started going after the growing indigenous rights activism, particularly the American Indian Movement organization.

Equally important, the FBI stepped aside in the midst of escalating violence against Black people—and Black activists in particular—casting white racist violence as a problem outside its jurisdiction, even when it witnessed the violence or had inside information. The FBI had monitored the Montgomery bus boycott back in the 1950s, but it appeared unconcerned with the bombing of the boycott leaders' homes. It also had early knowledge of forthcoming violence against the Freedom Riders but stepped aside and just let it happen. The agency had an informant in the car that attacked Viola Liuzzo, the white Detroit woman who was killed after the Selma to Montgomery March. But rather than risk the bad publicity, the FBI fumbled the investigation of her murder and spread ugly rumors about Liuzzo to discredit her.

The civil rights movement was ongoing, and its victories were hard-won, but the FBI's inaction served to boost and authorize violence against the hardworking people fighting for freedom.

# CHAPTER TWENTY-SIX

# "FREEDOM FIGHTERS NEVER RETIRE"

Rosa Parks had developed the ability to keep on keeping on, even amid personal hardship.

In 1972, Raymond was diagnosed with throat cancer. Rosa's brother and mother were also sick. Rosa's ulcers continued to plague her, and she developed heart trouble. "There was a time when I was traveling every day to three hospitals to visit them." This took a lot out of her, and she cut back her work at Conyers's office to part-time.

After a five-year battle with cancer, Raymond died on August 19, 1977, at the age of seventy-four. Three months later, her brother, Sylvester, died at the age of sixty-two.

"Words can't explain the double loss I felt," she said. "It was a sad and sorrowful time."

Then, two years later, her mother, Leona, died.

Rosa had suffered a string of immense losses. With all the illness and Raymond's death, she also struggled financially. She and Raymond had never been able to buy a house—and now her finances were even more strained. Parks considered retiring to Alabama, where it was warmer, but she couldn't afford to move back. Many people offered to raise money for her, but none of the good intentions fully materialized. As Parks had in the past, she drew on her inner resources of perseverance and faith, and she soldiered on. Parks was committed to freedom, and even these enormous losses wouldn't stop her. At an event honoring a fellow activist, Parks stated: "Freedom fighters never retire."

Part of Parks's ability to continue on came from the self-care practices she implemented. In 1965, she began doing yoga, attending classes with her nieces and nephews and practicing yoga at home. She kept up her yoga practice for the next three decades. Her niece Sheila said, "It was remarkable how she could adjust and adapt to new habits." In the 1960s, Parks had eagerly joined a new food co-op; later, she became a vegetarian to further improve her health.

Rosa Parks's vision of peace and human rights also encompassed a profound interest in other religious traditions. In 1992, she met Buddhist philosopher and educator Daisaku Ikeda and became interested in learning more about the peace traditions of Buddhism. On Ikeda's invitation, she journeyed to Japan in May 1994—her first cross-oceanic journey. (Her international travel to this point had only included Mexico and Canada.) The reaction to her in Japan was electric—the people and the media loved her. She was thrilled by the visit and the people she met. It was an experience of a lifetime. The deeper exposure to Buddhism led her to add meditation to her daily spiritual life of prayer and Bible reading. Parks's Christian faith, which had sustained her throughout her life, was enriched by learning from the traditions of other faiths.

■   ■   ■

P arks had long believed civil rights in America were inextricably linked with human rights abroad. The ways people of color were mistreated at home had clear parallels with how the United States treated countries of nonwhite people abroad. When the United States over-spent on war and military adventures around the world, that money was taken away from social programs that desperately needed funding at home. And, often, US fears of Communism led to the country supporting nondem-ocratic governments around the world—so long as they were anti-Communist.

One of the issues that moved Rosa Parks in the 1980s was US support for the racist government of South Africa. The country had instituted a legalized system of segrega-tion called apartheid. White people controlled the polit-ical, economic, and social structure of South Africa, as well as the police and the courts. And the United States was one of South Africa's strongest allies and business partners. Racial justice activists understood how US money was helping uphold the unjust South African system. They began a campaign calling on US businesses to divest from South Africa. Rosa Parks took part in the divestment movement, traveling the country and picketing outside the South African Embassy, in Washington, DC.

Parks was also critical of US foreign policy in Cen-tral America and the ways the United States intervened

Protesting apartheid outside the
South African embassy

to protect its own interests rather than the human rights of local people. The United States supported a brutal but anti-Communist government in El Salvador while attempting to unseat a democratically elected but socialist government in Nicaragua. Parks agreed to take part in a War Crimes Tribunal in 1984 hosted by the Center for Constitutional Rights, which sought to expose the human rights abuses the United States was committing throughout Latin America.

Three months after he was released from a South African prison in 1990, anti-apartheid leader Nelson Mandela visited the United States. He wanted to encourage a growing US anti-apartheid movement and increase the country's economic pressure on South Africa. Mandela met with President George H. W. Bush and traveled to eight cities. One of his stops was Detroit. A number of politicians and other dignitaries were invited to meet Mandela at the airport—but not Rosa Parks. However, once federal judge Damon Keith realized she'd been left off the invite list, he was horrified at the oversight and stopped by her home that morning to pick her up and take her. At first, she was embarrassed to go, but Judge Keith wouldn't take no for an answer, so off they went.

Mandela stepped off the plane. And then he saw Rosa Parks. Ignoring all the dignitaries and politicians who'd assembled to meet him, he walked straight toward her and began chanting, "Rosa Parks, Rosa Parks, Rosa Parks!" The two freedom fighters embraced.

John Conyers thought, "Rosa Parks is worldwide."

■    ■    ■

After Ronald Reagan became president in 1981, Parks grew discouraged by the ways his administration began undoing many of the changes they had fought for. She warned that if people didn't keep organizing, the "forces at work" would "destroy gains [that] have been made."

Parks was thrilled when Jesse Jackson, one of Dr. King's associates, decided to run for the Democratic nomination for president in 1984. Excited as she had been with Shirley Chisholm about the possibility of the first Black president, she headlined fundraisers and turned out for rallies for him. He did not win the nomination. She supported Jackson four years later, when he tried again, joining him onstage at the Democratic National Convention in 1988. Once more, she was saddened when he didn't receive the Democratic nomination.

When African American judge Clarence Thomas was nominated by President George H. W. Bush in 1991 to the Supreme Court to replace Thurgood Marshall (the first Black Supreme Court justice and a hero of Rosa Parks's), she felt she had to speak out against it. While she praised Thomas for his educational and professional successes, she noted his poor history with civil rights. She thought his appointment "would not represent a step forward on the road to racial progress but a U-turn on that road," and called on the Senate *not* to confirm him.

Closer to home, she continued to press for school equality and desegregation. After the nearly all-white suburb of Dearborn, Michigan, passed an ordinance saying that only residents could use its parks, Detroit NAACP activist Joe Madison and Rosa Parks started to organize for a boycott of Dearborn. But on the eve of the boycott, the city rescinded the ordinance.

By the 1980s and 1990s, Rosa Parks's long history of activism was being increasingly recognized. And for a shy person like Parks, this wasn't always easy. As she had since the day of her arrest on the bus, Parks found fame hard to deal with. People constantly wanted to talk about that one day back in December 1955. But for Rosa, it was like having to "pull off a scab over and over." She also found it annoying that people reduced her resistance to segregation to tired feet when her feet were never the problem—the problem was injustice. She was "weary of telling the story, weary of the reporters, weary of the questions." And she didn't like that she was only known for that day on the bus when she held a lifetime of political experiences.

On September 9, 1996, President Bill Clinton presented Rosa Parks with the Presidential Medal of Freedom. Three years later, in 1999, she received the nation's highest recognition, a Congressional Gold Medal. All but one congressman, Texas Republican Ron Paul, voted to bestow Parks with the reward; the vote in the Senate was unanimous.

Many of these honors turned Parks into a symbol of the past when she continued to insist there was so much more work to be done *in the present*. She was invited to speak at many events around the country, and she felt that talking about the movement was a way to keep the struggle going so she agreed to go. But often her work was relegated to distant history. "People equate me with Harriet Tubman and Sojourner Truth and ask if I knew them," she explained dejectedly. (Tubman, who escaped slavery and served as an Underground Railroad conductor and a Union spy, had been born *ninety-three years* before Parks. Sojourner Truth, who'd also escaped slavery, and had become an abolitionist writer and speaker, had died thirty years before Parks was even born.)

In 1988, Parks retired from John Conyers's office. Two years later, on her seventy-seventh birthday, the Kennedy Center in Washington, DC, hosted a gala concert in Rosa Parks's honor. A string of performers came out to celebrate her, including Lou Rawls, Dionne Warwick, Melissa Manchester, and Sister Sledge. Parks wore a beautiful pink lace evening gown. But she appeared to grow tired of all the love songs and flowery tributes. At the end of the evening, when it was her turn to talk, she spoke forcefully about how "we're still oppressed today."

In 1995, Parks, along with Queen Mother Moore and Betty Shabazz, the widow of Malcolm X, traveled to Washington, DC, to participate in the Million Man March, a march of African American men called for by Nation of Islam leader Louis Farrakhan. Many of her friends, particularly women friends, urged her not to go. But the young men organizing it had asked her to come, and so she said yes. Parks had long believed that if people felt she could be helpful, she'd be there.

Ironically, Parks gave a speech at the Million Man March when that wasn't even an option at the March on Washington in 1963. Greeted with an extraordinary ovation from the crowd, Rosa spoke about Raymond's role in the struggle and how she was "honored that young men respect me and have invited me as an elder."

# CHAPTER TWENTY-SEVEN

# THE STRUGGLE CONTINUES

Rosa Parks's bus stand may be her most famous act of courage, but another came much later—at the age of eighty-one.

On August 30, 1994, Parks was mugged in her home by a young man named Joseph Skipper. He snuck into her house, told her he'd prevented a burglar from robbing her, and asked for a tip. She went upstairs to retrieve her purse and gave him three dollars. But Skipper actually wanted all of her money. When Parks refused, Skipper became angry and hit her. He didn't seem to recognize her.

A lifelong believer in self-defense, the elderly Parks tried to defend herself. "Even at eighty-one years of age, I felt it was my right to defend myself!" He hit her again on the face and threatened to hurt her further. She ended up bruised and a bit battered—and badly shaken. And Skipper took her money.

Detroit residents were furious; Skipper was found and beaten before being turned over to the police. He was ultimately given an eight-to-fifteen-year prison sentence for assaulting and robbing Parks along with two other elderly women.

Many commentators latched onto the story and used it to chastise "the problems with Black youth today." The media framed Skipper as an example of a whole generation of Black youth who had gone astray from the values of their elders. So did many older African American people. To them, Rosa Parks being mugged was proof of how low Black youth had sunk.

Rosa Parks rejected this way of thinking. While she was quite shaken and saddened by the mugging, she didn't see what Skipper had done as a symbol of the problems with this new generation. Instead, she continued to stress the "conditions that produce violence." While gains had been made, she felt there were still more hurdles to overcome, as Black people still didn't have fair and equal treatment by the police, in schools, or in jobs. Parks was worried for Skipper's safety in prison, so she put out the word to people—including prisoners she knew—that he shouldn't be touched.

This incident, much like her bus arrest, revealed her inner strength and character. Unlike some people of her generation, she refused to treat Black youth as the problem and continued to place her hopes for change in the spirit and leadership of young people. She knew the conditions that produced unemployment, police brutality, and school inequality were what needed to be changed.

■　■　■

**M**rs. Park was clear: the struggle continued. In 1987, worried that adults were "too complacent," Parks cofounded the Rosa and Raymond Parks Institute for Self Development with longtime friend Elaine Steele to help young people carry the struggle forward.

She'd met Steele twenty-five years earlier, when the sixteen-year-old Steele briefly worked at Stockton Sewing Company alongside Parks. Steele was deeply political, like Mrs. Parks. It was through Steele and her political connections to the Republic of New Afrika in the late 1960s that Parks became friends with Robert and Mabel Williams. That shared political spirit was precious, and the two women developed a deep friendship. Over time, Steele came to be Parks's travel companion and grew to

Parks doodled on a pharmacy bag.

be like family, living across the street from her for many years and looking out for her.

The Rosa Parks Institute aimed to develop youth leadership and teach Black history. Parks had long placed her trust in young people to bring a spirit for change that would break through to the country. Her institute embodied this goal of youth leadership development. As a young person, Parks had discovered the power and strength of Black history—and so an intensive immersion in Black history was also part of the institute's early goals. The institute sent young people both south and north through its "Pathways to Freedom" program to learn Black history, including a tour of Underground Railroad sites. They emphasized the need to learn Black history "as early as [children] can learn anything," and provided college assistance, since one of Parks's greatest regrets was never having gone to college.

As much as her health permitted, she continued to push the struggle forward. Honored in Philadelphia in 1988, she stressed the need to keep fighting to ensure a better future for young people. She also made clear that older leaders and activists needed to take their cues from younger ones. "At some point we should step aside and let the younger ones take over. But we first must take care of our young people to make sure that they have the rights of first-class citizens."

As part of that belief, with the help of writer Jim Haskins, she wrote an autobiography geared toward young people, called *Rosa Parks: My Story*: "Many people have written their own versions of my life. . . . But when I tell my own story, then I know that is my own life." Parks wanted to set the record straight.

Up till the end of her life, Rosa Parks constantly told people the movement was not over and that there was much more work to be done. In 1999, she met Pope John Paul II, and she stressed to him how racism still plagued the world and needed continued challenging.

When she died, in October 2005, the tributes and national honors increased. She was the first nongovernment official and first woman ever to lie in honor in the Capitol Building. President George W. Bush ordered a statue of Rosa Parks to be placed in the Capitol's National Statuary Hall.

Eight years later, President Barack Obama joined with Democratic and Republican leaders to preside over the statue's unveiling. The group celebrated her "singular act of courage," repeated the myth that "she was tired so . . . she sat down," and used the event to proclaim what a great country the United States is. On that very same day, across town, the Supreme Court was hearing a voting rights case, *Shelby County v. Holder*; later that spring, the court eliminated key voting rights protections that Parks and her comrades had fought for decades to ensure. The Supreme Court found these voting protections no longer "relevant to present day."

So, while a statue was deemed important and relevant,

The statue of Rosa Parks in the Capitol. What does the statue convey? What might be missing?

that was not the case when it came to safeguarding the voting rights Parks and her fellow activists had fought to implement. And Parks was honored in ways that didn't do justice to her life history of freedom fighting or her ongoing belief in the need for continued struggle.

So why do we get the "tired bus lady" version when that story isn't true?

The ways that Rosa Parks is honored today—this master narrative—too often strips her of her substance and her boldness and the civil rights movement of its variety of organizers. It misses the movement's tenacity against the forces arrayed against it, and the decades of effort people like Parks put forward. She is reduced to a Black History Month poster or a Snapchat filter for International Women's Day.

This distorted version traps her story on the bus and misses her long history of fighting racism in the South *and* in the North. It places her struggle in the distant past, making it appear as though the problems of racism have been solved, when many of the issues Rosa was fighting for—like criminal justice, economic equity, desegregation of schools, Black history in the curriculum, and voting rights—are still ongoing needs in the United States today.

It makes it seem like a single act changed history when, instead, it was a lifetime of work by Rosa Parks and a community of people—not simply one or two great individuals. The movement following her arrest didn't just happen. It took an accumulation of bus resistance, failed attempt after failed attempt, and a group of activists who provided solace, vision, and further perseverance who kept going for years when there was nothing to suggest change was possible to actually build and carry out the civil rights movement. She persisted—and it is the story of that vision, perseverance, and collective struggle that must be told.

Too often, the ways she and Dr. King are honored are turned into a national redemption story. It becomes a tale of American progress to make us feel good about ourselves as a country, in the process papering over present-day injustice. And it puts a great distance between the civil rights movement and contemporary struggles like Black Lives Matter. Many commentators today hold up this fable of the civil rights movement to chastise and correct contemporary movements like Black Lives Matter, saying that young activists today are too extreme, unreasonable, and disruptive. They miss that such criticisms were directed against Parks, King, and the civil rights movement too—but they pressed forward anyway.

Parks spent her life fighting the injustices of the criminal justice system, including police brutality, the over-incarceration of Black people, and the lack of protection for Black people from white violence. Throughout her life, she stood with young people challenging inequality and injustice, holding out her greatest hope for change in their bold spirit. And she believed in the power of direct action and the need to disrupt unjust systems. So where would she be standing today?

Perhaps most troublingly, the paper-doll version of Rosa Parks reflects a view of the movement as completed when the actual Rosa Parks believed young people needed to carry it forward. This portrayal makes it seem like we couldn't possibly do what she and other civil rights activists did—when over and over, Rosa Parks insisted we could.

As she reminded Spelman College students, "Don't give up and don't say the movement is dead."

I began my career after college teaching three classes of African American history at the Jeremiah Burke High School, a segregated public school in Boston with an amazing principal. My students showed me the power and the joy of having access to learning Black history in high school. Partly because of their influence and encouragement, I went on to graduate school and became a professor, but I have worked with high school students in various capacities since. Since my original biography of Rosa Parks came out, I have repeatedly been asked to adapt it for younger readers, and so this book feels like I'm returning to where I started: to give young adults a rigorous, expansive African American history and the tools for questioning how American history is often told and taught.

I am tremendously grateful to a host of people who have helped me write this book, especially Brandy Colbert; Say Burgin; Jesse Hagopian and his students at Garfield High School—Bethel Getu, Roslena Hoard, Ke'Von Avery, Chardonnay Beaver, Janelle Gary, Umoya McKinney, and Khabirah Weddington; Chitra Aiyar, Jenna Carter Johnson, and the students of Sadie Nash Leadership Summer Program; Deborah Menkart, Bill Bigelow, and the Zinn Education Project; Francis Gourrier; Lisa Eboigbe; Eve Ewing; Val Brown and the educators of #CleartheAir; Taylor McGraw and the activists of Teens Take Charge; Brian Jones; Ansley Erickson; Adrienne

Cannon; Meg McAleer; Erik Wallenberg; Joshua Clark Davis; my editor for the original book, Gayatri Patnaik; Olivia Bauer, Will Myers, and Alison Rodriguez, who did photo research; Louis Roe for the beautiful cover; Susan Lumenello, Marcy Barnes, and Kim Arney for the care in producing this book; and my editor for this book, Joanna Green, for her excitement about bringing this history to young people.

A circle of scholar-activist-friends have lifted up me and this work on Rosa Parks over and again. I am grateful for Marwa Amer, Dayo Gore, Mary Phillips, Melissa Harris Perry, Aviva Stahl, Arun Kundnani, Sally Eberhardt, Pardiss Kebriaei, Faisal Hashmi, Robin Kelley, LisaGay Hamilton, Angela Sadler Williamson, Jessica Murray, Bryan Stevenson, the 2015 NEH "Jim Crow North" summer seminar, Pam Horowitz, the late Julian Bond, the late Gwen Ifill, Johanna Hamilton, Yoruba Richen, Henry Louis Gates, Bennett Ashley, Matthew Delmont, Joseph Entin, Alan Aja, and Dominick Braswell.

None of this would be possible without my community of friends and family who have loved Rosa Parks with me since I began this work fifteen years ago: Alejandra Marchevsky, Jason Elias, Emilio Elias Marchevsky, Arnold Franklin, Prudence Cumberbatch, Karen Miller, Brian Purnell, Komozi Woodard, Stephanie Melnick, Brenda Cardenas, Liz Theoharis, George Theoharis, Sam Theoharis, Ella Theoharis, Chris Caruso, Sophia Theoharis Caruso, Luke Theoharis Caruso, and Nancy and Athan Theoharis.

Most of the citations for the quotes and other references in this book can be found in Jeanne Theoharis, *The Rebellious Life of Mrs. Rosa Parks* (Boston: Beacon Press, 2015).

### Websites for Teaching and Learning About Rosa Parks

*RosaParksBiography.org*, by Jeanne Theoharis, Say Burgin, and Jessica Murray. Much of the material found on the web on Rosa Parks is limited and problematic, so we built this website to highlight Parks's entire life history of activism, particularly around criminal justice, with relevant primary sources, a timeline of her life and political work, and teachers' guides.

*Zinnedproject.org/rosa-parks-lesson*, by Bill Bigelow and the Zinn Education Project. This lesson in the form of a mixer activity introduces students to the variety of experiences and political work Rosa Parks engaged in.

*Beacon.org/rosaparksguide*. This teachers' guide by Val Brown of #CleartheAir, crafted especially for this book, helps educators use Rosa Parks's full history in the classroom.

### Other Key Texts

Brinkley, Douglas. *Rosa Parks: A Life*. New York: Penguin, 2000.

Kohl, Herb. *She Would Not Be Moved: How We Tell the Story of Rosa Parks and the Montgomery Bus Boycott*. New York: New Press, 2007.

McGuire, Danielle. *At the Dark End of the Street: Black Women, Rape and Resistance—A New History of the Civil Rights Movement from Rosa Parks to the Rise of Black Power*. New York: Knopf, 2010.

Parks, Rosa, with James Haskins. *Rosa Parks: My Story.* New York: Dial Books, 1992.

Rosa Parks Collection. Manuscripts Division, Library of Congress, Washington, DC. Online at https://www.loc.gov /collections/rosa-parks-papers/about-this-collection.

Rosa Parks Papers, Walter Reuther Library, Wayne State University, Detroit, MI.

Theoharis, Jeanne. *A More Beautiful and Terrible History: The Uses and Misuses of Civil Rights History.* Boston: Beacon Press, 2018.

### Notable Interviews of Rosa Parks

Anderson, Trezzvant. "How Has the Dramatic Bus Boycott Affected Montgomery Negroes?" Second article in series in *Pittsburgh Courier*, November 16, 1957.

Dannett, Sylvia. *Profiles of Negro Womanhood, Volume 2.* Yonkers, NY: Educational Heritage, 1966.

Parks, Rosa. Interview. Rosa Parks File, Box 2 File 7, George Metcalf Paper. Schomburg Center for Research on Black Culture of the New York Public Library, New York, NY.

Parks, Rosa. Interview with Blackside, Inc. November 14, 1985. For *Eyes on the Prize: America's Civil Rights Years (1954–1965).* Available at Washington University Digital Library, http://digital.wustl.edu/eyesontheprize.

Parks, Rosa. Interview with John H. Britton, September 28, 1967, Civil Rights Documentation Project, Moorland Spingarn at Howard University.

Parks, Rosa. Interview for *You Got to Move.* Folder 24, Lucy Massie Phenix Collection, State Historical Society of Wisconsin, Madison, WI.

Poinsett, Alex. "The Troubles of the Bus Boycott's Forgotten Woman." *Jet*, July 14, 1960.

Rovetch, Emily, ed. *Like It Is: Arthur E. Thomas Interviews Leaders on Black America.* New York: E. P. Dutton, 1981.

Selby, Earl, and Miriam Selby. *Odyssey: Journey Through Black America.* New York: G. P. Putnam, 1971.

Wigginton, Eliot. *Refuse to Stand Silently By: An Oral History of Grassroots Social Activism in America, 1921–1964.* New York: Anchor, 1991.

**Autobiographies and Biographies of Rosa Parks's Montgomery Comrades**

Branch, Taylor. *Parting the Waters: America in the King Years, 1954–1963*. New York: Simon & Schuster, 1988.

Burks, Mary Fair. "Trailblazers: Women in the Montgomery Bus Boycott." In *Women in the Civil Rights Movement: Trailblazers and Torchbearers, 1941–1965*. Edited by Vicki L. Crawford, Jacqueline Anne Rouse, and Barbara Woods. Bloomington: Indiana University Press, 1993.

Durr, Virginia Foster. *Outside the Magic Circle: The Autobiography of Virginia Foster Durr*. Montgomery: University of Alabama Press, 1985.

Garrow, David. *The Walking City: The Montgomery Bus Boycott, 1955–1956*. Brooklyn, NY: Carlson, 1989.

Graetz, Robert. *A White Preacher's Memoir: The Montgomery Bus Boycott*. Montgomery: Black Belt Press, 1998.

Gray, Fred. *Bus Ride to Justice: Changing the System by the System*. Montgomery: New South, 2002.

Hoose, Phillip. *Claudette Colvin: Twice Toward Justice*. New York: Farrar, Straus & Giroux, 2009.

King, Martin Luther, Jr. *Stride Toward Freedom: The Montgomery Story*. Originally published 1958. Boston: Beacon Press, 2010.

Robinson, Jo Ann Gibson. *The Montgomery Bus Boycott and the Women Who Started It: The Memoir of Jo Ann Gibson Robinson*. Knoxville: University of Tennessee Press, 1987.

Stanton, Mary. *Journey Toward Justice: Juliette Hampton Morgan and the Montgomery Bus Boycott*. Athens: University of Georgia Press, 2006.

Sullivan, Patricia, ed. *Freedom Writer: Virginia Foster Durr, Letters from the Civil Rights Years*. New York: Routledge, 2003.

Williams, Donnie, with Wayne Greenshaw. *The Thunder of Angels: The Montgomery Bus Boycott and the People Who Broke the Back of Jim Crow*. Chicago: Lawrence Hill, 2006.

**Key Sources on Black Politics in Alabama in the Decades Before and During the Montgomery Bus Boycott**

Gilmore, Glenda. *Defying Dixie: The Radical Roots of Civil Rights 1919–1950*. New York: W. W. Norton, 2008.

Kelley, Robin D. G. *Hammer and Hoe: Alabama Communists During the Great Depression*. Chapel Hill: University of North Carolina Press, 1990.

Thornton, J. Mills, III. *Dividing Lines: Municipal Politics and the Struggle for Civil Rights in Montgomery, Birmingham, and Selma.* Montgomery: University of Alabama Press, 2002.

### Autobiographies and Biographies of Rosa Parks's Comrades Around the Country

Charron, Katherine Mellen. *Freedom's Teacher: The Life of Septima Clark.* Chapel Hill: University of North Carolina Press, 2009.

Clark, Septima, with Cynthia Stokes Brown. *Ready from Within: Septima Clark and the Civil Rights Movement.* Navarro, CA: Wild Trees Press, 1986.

D'Emilio, John. *Lost Prophet: The Life and Times of Bayard Rustin.* NY: Free Press, 2003.

Farmer, Ashley. *Remaking Black Power: How Women Transformed an Era.* Durham: University of North Carolina Press, 2017.

Gore, Dayo. *Radicalism at the Crossroads: African American Women Activists in the Cold War.* New York: New York University Press, 2011.

Horton, Myles. *The Long Haul: An Autobiography.* New York: Teachers College Press, 1997.

Ransby, Barbara. *Ella Baker and the Black Freedom Movement.* Chapel Hill: University of North Carolina Press, 2002.

Scanlon, Jennifer. *Until There is Justice: The Life of Anna Arnold Hedgeman.* New York: Oxford University Press, 2016.

Tyson, Timothy B. *Radio Free Dixie: Robert F. Williams and the Roots of Black Power.* Chapel Hill: University of North Carolina Press, 1999.

### Key Autobiographies and Histories of Black Detroit

Dillard, Angela. *Faith in the City: Preaching Radical Social Change in Detroit.* Ann Arbor: University of Michigan Press, 2007.

Fine, Sidney. *Violence in the Model City: The Cavanagh Administration, Race Relations, and the Detroit Riot of 1967.* Ann Arbor: University of Michigan Press, 1989.

Hampton, Henry. *Voices of Freedom: An Oral History of the Civil Rights Movement from the 1950s through the 1980s.* New York: Bantam, 1990.

Johnson, Arthur. *Race and Remembrance: A Memoir.* Detroit: Wayne State University Press, 2008.

Mast, Robert. *Detroit Lives.* Philadelphia: Temple University Press, 1994.

Miller, Karen. *Managing Inequality: Northern Racial Liberalism in Interwar Detroit.* New York: New York University Press, 2014.

Moon, Elaine Latzman. *Untold Tales, Unsung Heroes: An Oral History of Detroit's African American Community, 1918–1967.* Detroit: Wayne State University Press, 1994.

Purnell, Brian, Jeanne Theoharis, and Komozi Woodard, eds. *The Strange Careers of the Jim Crow North: Segregation and Struggle Outside of the South.* New York: New York University Press, 2019.

Smith, Suzanne. *Dancing in the Streets: Motown and the Cultural Politics of Black Detroit.* Cambridge, MA: Harvard University Press, 2001.

Sugrue, Thomas J. *The Origins of the Urban Crisis: Race and Inequality in Postwar Detroit.* Princeton, NJ: Princeton University Press, 1996.

Sugrue, Thomas. *Sweet Land of Liberty: The Forgotten Struggle for Civil Rights in the North.* New York: Knopf, 2008.

p.12, p.16, p.21, p.26, p.13, p.45, p.50, p.52, p.60, p.63, p.86, p. 102, p.133, p.145, p.146, p.172, p.237, p. 242, p.250, p.267: © Rosa Parks, used with permission from the Rosa and Raymond Parks Institute for Self Development.

p.18: New York Public Library.

p. 27: Library of Congress, Rare Book and Special Collections Division, Printed Ephemera Collection.

p.41: Alabama Department of Archives and History.

p.42: *Montgomery Advertiser.*

p. 48: CC BY-SA 3.0. Photographer Chris Pruitt.

p.70: Archive PL/Alamy Stock Photo.

p. 73: Courtesy of *Alabama Journal.*

p. 84: Wisconsin Historical Society, WHS-56318.

p.91: Everett Collection Historical/Alamy Stock Photo.

p.99: US National Archives.

p.109: Stanford University/MLK Institute.

p.119: AP Photo.

p.113: US National Archives record ID: 306-PSD-65-1882 (Box 93). Source: *Ebony Magazine.*

p.130: The LIFE Images Collection via Getty Images/Getty Images. Photo by Don Cravens.

p.131: AP Wide World.

p.139: Montgomery County Archives.

p.157: Courtesy of Asbury Park Evening Press.

p. 168: Courtesy of Home Owners' Loan Corporation.

p.169: Library of Congress, Prints and Photographs Division. Photography by Arthur S. Siegel.

p.179: Courtesy of Andrew Sacks/saxpix.com.

p.191: Stocktrek Images, Inc./Alamy Stock Photo.

p. 193: Courtesy of ©Bob Adelman Estate.

p.195: Source: Gallup.

p.201: Photograph by Daymon J. Hartley.

p.204: Walter P. Reuther Library, Archives of Labor and Urban Affairs, Wayne State University, Detroit, MI.

p.211: Photograph by LeRoy Henderson.

p.215: Everett Collection, Inc./Alamy Stock Photo.

p.216: Courtesy of Matt Heron/TakeStock, 1976.

p.223: Courtesy of Edward Vaughn.

p.231: Courtesy of Dorothy Aldridge.

p.239: Courtesy of the Library of Congress, Prints and Photographs Division. Photograph by Warren K. Leffl er, 1968.

p.247: Courtesy of Ericka Huggins Collection.

p.260: Photograph by Jim Hubbard.

p. 269: Courtesy of the Architect of the Capitol.

MLK in Boston, 93; and the PPC, 237; role in bus boycott, 134–35; speech at Solidarity Day, 238–39
King, Martin Luther, Jr.: assassination, 236, 240; attacks on the WCC, 214; background, education, 92; bombing of home, 134–35; conflicts with Nixon, 159; description of RP, 116; at the Dexter Avenue Baptist Church, 92, 112, 160; divinity studies, 93; eloquence, 94, 123–24, 193, 233; at the Great Walk for Freedom, 181; hostility towards, harassment, 62, 138, 214, 235–36; "master narrative" about, 5; middle class background, 95, 160; nothing easy about leadership role, 112; and the Poor People's Campaign, 237; relationship with RP, 95, 116, 161, 211; on rioting among Black, 230, 234; at the Selma to Montgomery March, 216; support for Conyers, 198–99; support for the bus boycott, 121, 123–24, 126–27, 138–40; surveillance by the FBI, 136–37, 196. *See also* civil rights movement; March on Washington for Jobs and Freedom; Southern Christian Leadership Conference (SCLC)
King, Rosalyn Oliver, 62
Ku Klux Klan (KKK), 11–13, 127, 152

Lackey, Drue, 140
Lee, George, 95

Lee, Prince, 189, 191
Lewis, John, 192–93, 214
Lewis, Rufus, 39
libraries, public, segregation in, 42, 59
Little, Earl, 206
Little, Joan, 7, 252–53
Little, Malcolm. *See* Malcolm X
Liuzzo, Viola, 217, 256
local politics, importance of electing Black candidates, 248–49
*Look* magazine, iconic photo of RP, 157–58
Lowndes County, Alabama, racist practices, 219–20
Lowndes County Freedom Organization, 218, 220–21. *See also* Carmichael, Stokely (Kwame Ture)
Lumumba, Chokwe, 253–54
Lumumba, Patrice, 177
lunch counter sit-ins, 182–85. *See also* civil rights movement; social activism; Student Nonviolent Coordinating Committee (SNCC)
lynching, 7, 15–16, 49, 90–92, 95–96

Malcolm X, 206–12. *See also* Black Power movement; Nation of Islam (NOI)
Mandela, Nelson, 260–61
March on Washington for Jobs and Freedom: attendance, police/government response, 189–91; controversy over lack of women speakers, 188–89, 192, 194; disapproval of and attacks on, 194–95; King's speech, 181, 193; organizing, goals, 187–88; sequestering of

Nation of Islam (NOI), 206
Negro League, 51
newspaper subscriptions, 248
New York City: bus boycott,
    impacts, 125; RP's first visit
    to, 147–49
Niebuhr, Reinhold, 92
Nixon, Edgar Daniel (E.D.):
    background, union work,
    35; and the Brotherhood
    of Sleeping Car Workers,
    35–36; conflicts with King,
    159; continuing activism,
    88; criticisms of, 44, 53,
    156; efforts to get clergy
    support for the boycott,
    112; health problems, 152;
    indictment and arrest,
    138–40; on the larger
    meaning of the bus boycott,
    158; profile in the *Chicago
    Defender*, 88; relationship
    with RP, 36, 54, 150–51,
    162; on RP's arrest and
    court hearing, 106, 119–20;
    search for a test case,
    74–77; views on women,
    43, 121; voter registration
    efforts, 35; work with the
    NAACP, 35, 37, 39–42,
    45–46, 48, 49–50, 53–54,
    65, 68–69, 88
NOI. *See* Nation of Islam (NOI)
nonviolent direct action: as
    King's strategy, 242; lunch
    counter sit-ins, 182–85,
    251; RP's support for,
    210–11
Noonan, Martha Norman,
    186
Northern cities: Black mi-
    gration to, 52, 166, 168,
    173, 217, 224; racism in,
    165–71, 173, 197, 200,

202–203, 222–25, 234–36;
    civil rights movement in
    177, 179–81, 205, 207–10,
    262. *See also* Detroit,
    Michigan

Obama, Barack, 1, 269
Organization of Afro-American
    Unity, 209

Paille, Robert, 232. *See* People's
    Tribunal, Detroit
Parks, Raymond: activism,/
    courage 27–31; background,
    education, 25–27; death,
    202, 257; education, 25–26;
    financial difficulties, 143,
    150–51, 171–72; frustra-
    tion over slow progress,
    34, 81; harassment/ death
    threats, 142–44, 162; health
    problems, 7, 151–52, 173,
    229; marriage to Rosa,
    29–30; and the Montgomery
    NAACP, 34; move to/home
    in Detroit, 162–63, 178;
    physical appearance, 25–26;
    support role, 49, 82, 106,
    254; registering to vote, 38,
    work as a barber, 62–63, 80,
    178. *See also* bus boycott,
    Montgomery
Parks, Rosa McCauley: as an
    "accidental" heroine, 5,
    127; burying/distorting
    of activist record, 1–2, 4,
    128, 156, 201, 270, 274;
    ambition/courage, 20,
    100–101; on the Detroit
    Riot/uprising, 225, 229;
    called a Communist,
    127–28, 214–15; childhood
    and formal education,
    17–18, 20; cooking and

police brutality: and the Detroit Riot, 225–26, 227, 230; Hilliard Brooks, 65–66; and the lack of protection for Blacks, 38–39, 55; organized resistance to, 180, 190, 207, 212, 232, 266, 271; and People's Tribunal, 230–32; and the rape of Black women, 50, 64; RP's activist challenges to, 7; and RP's thoughts on, 229–31; and the Scottsboro Boys, 28, 31; and violence towards Black people, 65, 71, 93–94, 214–15, 223–25, 253–55. See also bus boycott, Montgomery; lunch counter sit-ins

police brutality/killings: murder of Brooks, 65–66; and violence against arrested people and, 50; by Detroit police 224–25, 227, 230, 271 . See also violence against Black people

political prisoners, 251–54. See also FBI

Pollard, Aubrey, 227

poll taxes, 37–38

Poor People's Campaign (PPC), 237–40

Powell, Adam Clayton, Jr., 125

Presidential Medal of Freedom, 262

prison reform efforts, 55–56, 252–53

Progressive Democratic Association, 125

Project Z (FBI), 255

public housing, 47–48, 66, 150, 170

Pullman Company, 35–36

quilt-making traditions, 244

racism: among Northerners, King's criticisms of, 234; and Black political power, 50, 248; and bus segregation, 61–63; as cause of poverty, 239; and the causes of the Detroit Riot, 229–30; in daily life, emotional impacts, 14–16, 52, 59–62, 80; in Detroit, 52–53, 165–71, 190, 202–3, 222–25; and the Double V campaign, 33; and global rights, RP's work to promote, 259; impacts on lives of Black youth, 59; as a national problem, 165–66; need for ongoing struggle against, 263; and policing in Detroit, 224–25; and the slowness of change, 242; and the toll it takes, 240. See also Black Power movement; civil rights movement; Detroit, Michigan; white supremacy

Randolph, A. Philip, 147, 187, 189–92

rape. See Black women; violence against Black people

Reagan, Ronald, 261

red-lining practices, 167–68, 178

Red Summer, 11

Reese, Jeanetta, 156

Reeves, Jeremiah, 7, 55, 70

reparations, 193, 245, 253

Republic of New Afrika (RNA), 253–54

Resistance/activism: and the building up of multiple injustices, 77–78; RP's philosophy of resistance, 24

restrictive covenants, 168–70

Resurrection City, Washington, DC, 238, 240

Jeanne Theoharis is Distinguished Professor of Political Science at Brooklyn College of the City University of New York and the author or coauthor of nine books and numerous articles on the civil rights and Black Power movements, the politics of race and education, and social welfare and civil rights in post-9/11 America. Her widely acclaimed

biography *The Rebellious Life of Mrs. Rosa Parks* won a 2014 NAACP Image Award and the Letitia Woods Brown Award from the Association of Black Women Historians and appeared on the *New York Times* bestseller list. Her book *A More Beautiful and Terrible History: The Uses and Misuses of Civil Rights History* won the 2018 Brooklyn Public Library Literary Prize for Nonfiction. Her work has appeared in the *New York Times*, the *Washington Post*, MSNBC, *The Nation*, *The Root*, *Slate*, *The Intercept*, and the *Chronicle of Higher Education*. Connect with her on Twitter (@JeanneTheoharis).

**B**randy Colbert is the award-winning author of several books for children and teens, including *The Only Black Girls in Town*, *The Voting Booth*, and Stonewall Book Award winner *Little & Lion*. She is co-writer of Misty Copeland's *Life in Motion* young readers' edition, and her short fiction and essays have been published in a variety of critically acclaimed anthologies for young people. Her books have been chosen as Junior Library Guild selections, and have appeared on many best of lists, including the American Library Association's Best Fiction for Young Adults and Quick Picks for Reluctant Young Adult Readers. She is on faculty at Hamline University's MFA program in writing for children, and lives in Los Angeles.

Photo credit: Jessie Weinberg